DEFENSE, SECURITY AND STRATEGIES

LANDPOWER IN THE 21ST CENTURY

PERSPECTIVES ON POLICY AND STRATEGY

DEFENSE, SECURITY AND STRATEGIES

Additional books in this series can be found on Nova's website under the Series tab.

Additional e-books in this series can be found on Nova's website under the e-book tab.

DEFENSE, SECURITY AND STRATEGIES

LANDPOWER IN THE 21ST CENTURY

PERSPECTIVES ON POLICY AND STRATEGY

ELIZABETH BAKER
EDITOR

New York

Library of Congress Cataloging-in-Publication Data

ISBN: 978-1-63483-172-7

Published by Nova Science Publishers, Inc. † New York

CONTENTS

PREFACE

Landpower, defined here as "the ability—by threat, force, or occupation—to exploit control over land, resources, and people," offers policymakers significant utility in peace, crisis, or war. This book provides better understanding of Landpower essential if national leaders are to have a full range of policy options for protecting and promoting the nation's interests in the face of shifting geostrategic conditions.

In: Landpower in the 21st Century
Editor: Elizabeth Baker
ISBN: 978-1-63483-172-7

Chapter 1

RE-EXAMINING THE ROLES OF LANDPOWER IN THE 21ST CENTURY AND THEIR IMPLICATIONS*

William T. Johnsen

ABSTRACT

Much has happened in the 16 years since this author penned a monograph entitled *Redefining Land Power for the 21st Century*. The United States suffered the tragedies of September 11, 2001, the first attack of a wave of large-scale extremist terrorist activities that have scourged the globe from London to Bali to Madrid to Mumbai to Nairobi and beyond. The invasion and subsequent counterinsurgency campaigns in Iraq and the ebbing war in Afghanistan have significantly engaged U.S. military power, especially Landpower, for over a decade. The ongoing volatility of the international security environment continues to generate crises that may embroil U.S. national interests: an increasingly erratic North Korea that may be on the verge of implosion, confrontation with Iran over its nuclear policies, the turbulence of the Arab Spring and its consequences, growing unrest in broad swaths of Africa, and multiple crises in the Middle East, to name but a few. Moreover, the dramatic rise of China as a global economic and regional military power and a

* This is an edited, reformatted and augmented version of a monograph issued by the Strategic Studies Institute, November 2014.

resurgent and revanchist Russia could lead to renewed great power competition.

The character of warfare has undergone significant change, as well. Accelerating technological innovation, whether in new weapons or dramatically increased precision of older weapons, continues to revolutionize warfare. At the same time, the return of older forms of warfare, such as guerilla warfare and insurgencies, further complicate the conduct of modern war. The rise of nonstate actors with weapons that can exceed the capabilities of many states has emerged as a new factor. All of this in combination has led, supposedly, to new forms of warfare, such as hybrid warfare or 4th Generation Warfare, that have increased the complexity of modern warfare. Lastly, the rise of cyber-based capabilities has yet to reveal the full extent of what may be an entirely new battlefield. All told, the character of warfare has changed remarkably, and will undoubtedly continue to do so.

Yet, numerous continuities remain. By the late-1990s, the American public already had grown tired of prolonged peacekeeping and nation-building operations in Africa and the Balkans.[1] Trying to bring democracy to the Middle East and Southwest Asia over the course of the last decade-plus has proven too expensive in terms of lives and treasure lost relative to perceived gains. The U.S. withdrawal from Iraq at the end of 2011 and the denouement of the war in Afghanistan have left a war weary U.S. public. Moreover, just as after the U.S. withdrawal from Vietnam, prolonged counterinsurgencies in Afghanistan and Iraq—with a heavy commitment of ground forces—has dulled any American appetite for further participation in counterinsurgency operations.[2]

Like the 1990s, rising fiscal pressures have accompanied this general disillusionment with U.S. global engagement. Political and military leaders have expressed concern that the number one priority for the United States is getting its fiscal house in order.[3] At the same time, the United States is in the midst of executing a geo-strategic "rebalance" to the Asia-Pacific region, an expensive undertaking. Budget constraints, particularly the rise of mandatory spending cuts, place increasing pressure on the Department of Defense budget.

These combined disenchantments have translated into a public leery of further interventions. While analysts and policymakers cannot know with certainty whether the U.S. public and political leadership will countenance any more "long wars," recent experience in Libya, strong opposition to U.S. involvement in the civil war in Syria, public apathy over the Russian seizure of parts of Ukraine, and indifference to renewed fighting in Iraq offer hints that future intervention may be difficult to undertake. Because of the confluence of all of these issues, some national leaders, defense intellectuals, and analysts have questioned once more the continuing relevance of land forces and Landpower. Thus, in an incredibly ironic paradox, after 13 years of wars fought largely within the human dimension predominantly by ground forces that have borne the brunt of combat and casualties, proponents of Landpower feel compelled to explain Landpower and justify the retention of Landpower capabilities in the face of significant budget (and, therefore force structure and personnel) cuts.

The combination of these circumstances call for a new examination of the roles of Landpower in the 21st century.

About the Author

WILLIAM T. JOHNSEN currently serves as Professor of Military History and Strategy in the Department of National Security and Strategy, U.S. Army War College. From 1991-99, he served in the Strategic Studies Institute, ultimately as Research Professor of National Security Affairs. He also held the Elihu Root Chair of Military Studies at the U.S. Army War College from 1994-97. In 1999, he became the inaugural Associate Dean for Academic Policy, while also serving as the Director, Department of Academic Affairs. In December 2002, he assumed the duties of Acting Dean of Academics. In June 2003, Dr. Johnsen became the Dean of Academics, serving in that position until June 2012. After a 1-year sabbatical leave, he assumed his current duties. In addition to his academic career, Professor Johnsen served as an Infantry officer for 20 years before retiring from the U.S. Army. In addition to a variety of troop leading, command, and staff assignments, he also served as an Assistant Professor of history at the U.S. Military Academy, and as an arms control analyst at Supreme Headquarters Allied Powers Europe (SHAPE). Dr. Johnsen has authored over 30 monographs, articles, or book chapters on U.S. and European security issues. His book, *Forging the Foundations of the Grand Alliance: U.S.-British Military Collaboration from the Panay Incident to Pearl Harbor, 1937- 1941*, is forthcoming. Dr. Johnsen holds a B.S. from the U.S. Military Academy and an M.A. and Ph.D. in history from Duke University. He also is a graduate of the Armed Forces Staff College and the U.S. Army War College.

Summary

After 13 years of prolonged ground combat, a weary American public is leery of further interventions requiring land forces. Shifting geo-strategic conditions, such as a revanchist Russia and a rising China, reinforce this reluctance. At the same time, technological innovation once more offers the chimera of war from a distance that does not endanger land forces.

Nonetheless, at some point, a highly volatile international security environment will place U.S. national interests at risk, requiring the use of military power. Given the increasing rise of interdependence among all components of military power (air, cyberspace, land, sea, and space), a better understanding of Land-power is essential if national leaders are to have a full range of policy options for protecting and promoting those interests.

Landpower, "the ability—by threat, force, or occupation—to gain, sustain, exploit control over land, resources, and people," stems from a country's geo-strategic conditions, economic power, population, form of government, and national will. The military elements of Landpower include a country's ground forces, the institutions that generate and sustain those forces, and the human dimension—intelligent, highly adaptable, and innovative individuals—so vital to the successful employment of Landpower.

Landpower offers policymakers tremendous utility in peace, crisis, or war, as it can defeat, deter, compel, reassure, engage, and support the nation. Within each of these roles, as well as across them, Landpower can carry out the broadest range of military operations. This versatility across the spectrum of conflict offers national leaders the greatest number of effective policy options.

* * *

> ... every age had its own kind of war, its own limiting conditions, and its own peculiar preconceptions. Each period, therefore, would have held its own theory of war...
>
> Carl von Clausewitz, *On War*[1]

> Landpower is the ability—by threat, force, or occupation—to gain, sustain, exploit control over land, resources, and people.
>
> *Army Doctrine Publication 1, The Army*[2]

INTRODUCTION

While some readers may be surprised to learn that an official definition of the term Landpower is a recent phenomenon, this circumstance may not be as odd as outside observers might think.[3] For many military practitioners, especially Soldiers and Marines, the concept of Landpower is so deeply ingrained that it is largely self-evident. It has existed since our first ancestors used their fists, rocks, and sticks to defend themselves from attacks by predatory neighbors. As a result, a several millennial-long understanding of land warfare exists. Indeed, key strategists and theorists, such as Sun Tzu, Niccolò Machiavelli, Clausewitz, and Antoine-Henri Jomini, would not have thought of war as anything other than the application of Landpower.

At the same time, a less than clear understanding of the elements of military power reinforces this tacit understanding of Landpower.[4] For example, while fleets and navies occasionally played vital roles throughout history, even major naval victories such as the Battle of the Virginia Capes in the American War of Independence, Trafalgar in the Napoleonic Wars, or Jutland in World War I, were adjuncts to the main events on land.[5] Even after American Alfred Thayer Mahan and Briton Sir Julian Corbett distilled the essence of a theory of sea or maritime power at the turn of the 20th century, command of the sea concerned (and still does) only a few nations and powers.[6]

There is even less historical experience with and, therefore, understanding of, the remaining elements of military power. Air power is a 20th century phenomenon. Giulio Douhet, Hugh Trenchard, William Mitchell, and other key contributors to the embryonic theory of air power could emerge only after the invention of the airplane.[7] Space is a late 20th century phenomenon, and cyberspace, while originating in the 20th century, is emerging in its own right only in the first decades of the 21st century. Neither of these last two elements of military power has yet found a consensus prophet.[8]

All of these conditions have reinforced the historical precedent of Landpower as the dominant element of military power. Since the latter half of the 20th century, however, new technologies and ways of employing those technologies have chipped away at that traditional understanding. While terms such as Military-Technical Revolution (MTR) or Revolution in Military Affairs (RMA) may now be passé, no one disputes the accelerating changes in military technology that have occurred during the wars in Iraq and Afghanistan. Nor does the pace of change appear to be slowing. These changes simultaneously and paradoxically blur the dividing lines between where, when, and how the elements of military power might be employed. As a result, the historical dominance of Landpower may no longer translate into a self-evident understanding of Landpower.

Oftentimes, loose terminology further compounds misunderstanding. For instance, while professional military and civilians tend to use the terms Landpower, armies, land forces, and land warfare interchangeably, these terms are not synonymous. Moreover, interpretation of these words, like beauty, often lies in the eye of the beholder, and Soldiers, Sailors, Airmen, and Marines frequently have different perceptions. Even within large segments of land forces, interpretations will vary considerably depending upon whether one is a Soldier or a Marine; has a strategic, operational, or tactical bias; is from a maneuver, operational support, or force sustainment branch; or serves in a particular unit or theater. These differing perspectives bleed over into official doctrine. While the Army has defined Landpower, an official Joint definition of Landpower still does not exist.[9] Thus, while the Army may have a particular view of Landpower, those outside the Army may not widely share that perspective.

The culmination of these factors too frequently results in divisive debates that reinforce convictions rather than clarify matters that help make U.S. military power and its land component more effective. If senior military and defense advisors are to help national leaders understand how best to orchestrate the growing interdependence of air, cyberspace, land, sea, and space power to promote and protect national interests, they must understand both the capabilities and limitations each power offers in conjunction with the other components of military power. The recent initiative of the Chief of Staff of the Army, the Commandant of the Marine Corps, and the Commander,

Special Operations Command to create the Strategic Landpower Task Force ". . . to study the application of landpower to achieve national objectives in the future," underscores this imperative.[10]

To that end, this monograph first places Landpower in an appropriate context. It then elaborates on the concept of Landpower. Third, the monograph identifies the national and military elements of Landpower. Next, it examines the potential roles and missions of Landpower in the 21st century, to include an assessment of the strategic and operational versatility of Landpower. To assist policymakers in making future decisions, this assessment includes the strengths and weaknesses of Landpower. Finally, the monograph offers conclusions to spark a more informed debate on the roles Landpower in the 21st century.

CONTEXT

Just as military power is but one instrument of national power, Landpower is but one element of military power. Military power combines with diplomatic, economic and informational power to form a whole, while Landpower works with air, cyberspace, sea and space power.[11] Moreover, at the strategic level, decisive results generally require orchestrating more than one element of military power, oftentimes in concert with other instruments of national power. Thus, despite the claims of their more extreme advocates, rarely will air, cyberspace, land, sea, or space power, alone, be sufficient to promote, let alone protect national interests. Granted, cases may arise where one form of military power may play a dominant role. However, for reasons explained more fully later, those occasions will be rare.

The term "conflict," as opposed to warfare, generally will appear in this monograph. Conflict is a broader term that better describes anticipated conditions that range from peacetime competition (e.g., economic rivalries, diplomatic friction, and ideological antagonisms) through general war (to include the use of weapons of mass destruction [WMD]). Conflict also encompasses a wide range of military operations indicated in Figure 1 that support U.S. national interests.

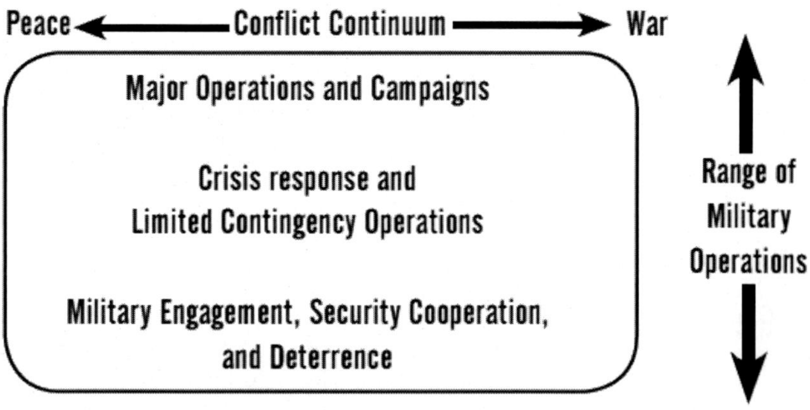

Figure 1. Range of Military Operations.[12] The Future Security Environment.

A detailed and predictive examination of the future security environment is unlikely to yield much gain. While leaders someday may be able to divine the distant future with precision, today is not likely to be that day. Nor is tomorrow. Despite spending billions of dollars, our foresight is constrained. As one senior leader recently observed, even "the foreseeable future isn't really foreseeable."[13] Similarly, former Secretary of Defense Robert Gates has often remarked that when it comes to predicting the future with precision, we have 100 percent accuracy—we have gotten zero right.[14] Worse, such a lack of clarity about the distant future security environment all too frequently leads to arguments over assumptions at the expense of the primary focus on the issue at hand. This is particularly true when engaging in debates over when and how to employ military power. For example, specific scenarios oftentimes quickly come under fire from those who do not agree on the need for X or Y conditions. Alternatively, critics may ridicule scenarios as fantasies or "laundry lists" used as a way to avoid a substantive discussion of the merits of a particular issue.

The foregoing is not an argument for not looking ahead. Forecasting is necessary, but one must avoid predictions that take focus away from the primary task. In this vein, the author offers a few general observations to establish a broad context of the future security environment that can facilitate an analysis of Landpower. First, despite our ardent desires, conflict is not going away. Long historical experience reinforces this fact, and current trends of the last 20-25 years indicate more of the same for the next 20-25 years. We also know from experience that unexpected security challenges are likely to erupt on little or no notice. The only forecast that has any degree of certainty is that somewhere, sometime in the coming years (undoubtedly not at the time of our choosing) some country, organization, nonstate actor, or combination thereof will place U.S. national security interests at sufficient risk to require a military response. When, where, and how that might occur is an open question, which means the United States is unlikely to have the luxury of planning against discrete security challenges. These uncertainties will require the United States to anticipate and prepare for a broad range of possible challenges.

In planning for such a range of outcomes, U.S. leaders would be wise to heed the sage advice of historian Sir Michael Howard, who years ago noted that getting things exactly right was less important (as well as less likely) than not getting things too wrong.[15] Regardless, U.S. political and military leaders also will have to hedge against unanticipated outcomes, the so-called "black swans" (such as using commercial airliners to attack buildings) that all too frequently arise.[16] Lastly, one should never forget that adversaries and competitors get a vote.

Military Elements of Power

As indicated earlier, the accepted elements or components of military power include air, cyberspace, land, sea, and space power. All five elements will remain relevant to future conflicts. The question is what might be the appropriate blend of the five. There is no current argument, compelling or otherwise, that the traditional dominant elements of land, sea, and air will fade from prominence any time soon. Nonetheless, space and cyberspace may take on larger roles than heretofore.

For example, while this author agreed 16 years ago that space overarched all physical domains, he argued that space had not yet achieved status as a full-fledged element of military power in its own right. The increasing dependence of modern military forces upon capabilities based in space have called that conclusion into question as the operations in the physical domain of space have assumed greater importance in peace, crisis, and war.[17] Thus, while space presently continues to serve predominantly as an enabler of the other elements of military power, it clearly has secured its place as a key element of military power. As space capabilities continue to evolve, air, cyberspace, land, and sea power may exploit the possibilities inherent in space, and use of space assets and capabilities undoubtedly will increase.

Similarly, the 1998 monograph argued that it was too soon to conclude definitively that cyberspace would soon become a discrete element of military power.[18] The time has come to reconsider that conclusion. On the one hand, cyberspace and the information that flows through it, like space, is a tool that supplements, complements, and, indeed, permeates all of the existing elements of national and military power. While cyberspace has its limits, costs, and potential consequences, it might soon become an element of military power in its own right if the virtual world and artificial intelligence continue along their current trajectories. Until such a time, national and military leaders will have to obtain as complete an understanding of cyberspace power and its strengths and weaknesses as possible to ensure cyberspace power continues to augment and enable the remaining elements of military power. Just like all elements of military power, cyberspace power cannot be an end unto itself.

INTERDEPENDENCE

The 1998 monograph posited that interdependence—then defined as "orchestrating the appropriate components of military power in ways that achieve desired results"—would increasingly become the norm for the U.S. military.[19] The original monograph argued that interdependence, as a concept, went beyond the then current scope of joint operations, which essentially sought close cooperation among the Services to achieve military and national objectives.[20] At the time, this author argued that interdependence would go beyond integration of Service capabilities to the point where Services would depend upon each other for the performance of the majority of the roles, missions, and tasks that national leaders call upon the Armed Forces of the United States to perform. That idea has been borne out by historical experience over the last 16 years. Indeed, military operations in Iraq and Afghanistan have raised interdependence from a hypothetical concept to a fact of modern U.S. warfare, as *Joint Publication TI, Doctrine of the U.S. Armed Forces*, now defines joint interdependence as "... the purposeful reliance by one Service on another Service's capabilities to maximize complementary and reinforcing effects of both (i.e., synergy), the degree of interdependence varying with specific circumstances."[21]

While this definition is a good first step, a better understanding of how interdependence has and will continue to evolve will be imperative for effective U.S. responses to the future demands of the 21st century security environment.[22] Only by thoroughly understanding of how Services and Special Operations Forces can contribute to air, cyberspace, land, sea, and space power will the U.S. military be able to maximize the effectiveness of interdependent operations. As importantly, anticipated budget constraints and demands of the international security environment will make interdependence a necessity.

One of the key tenets of interdependent operations is that no one element of military power (or its contributing Services) exists in isolation. Under this author's conception of interdependent operations, every element operates in multiple domains and supports the other elements. In interdependent operations, therefore, the question is not which element of military power to apply. Rather, the key question is, what is the most appropriate mix of elements given the circumstances, missions, and capabilities required? In other words, interdependence results from the synergy gained by appropriately orchestrating the elements of U.S. military (and national) power to influence an opponent at least cost. The metaphor of a tapestry best illustrates, perhaps, this concept. The respective elements of military power (and their contributing Services) represent the threads that make up the tapestry. Individual threads, while essential for creating the tapestry, cannot create a picture. Even collectively, a picture emerges only when the weaver works the threads in a carefully planned and executed pattern. Extending the metaphor to demonstrate the extensive capabilities inherent in interdependent operations of the Services, a weaver can weave any number of threads and patterns to create endless varieties of pictures.

Paradoxically, the future orchestration of these multiple capabilities will be both easier and harder as the clear distinctions between the elements of military power continue to blur. For example, from ancient times through the mid-20th century, states exercised sea power primarily against other ships. Granted, limited operations against coastal fortifications and ports, and amphibious operations occasionally occurred. However, the application of sea power on land was limited to a narrow coastal strip. Today, carrier based aviation and cruise missiles extend the reach of sea power asymmetrically deep into the hinterland and airspace of most states. Amphibious operations can reach well beyond shorelines to strike deep into littoral areas, as well. Thus, sea power extends into the air and land elements of military power.

Similarly, in its infancy, air power initially reconnoitered ground forces. Quickly, however, the ability to attack ground targets from the air opened up the possibility of influencing land combat.[23] Eventually, the range of aircraft permitted air forces to strike deep into an opponent's territory directly to attack its war making potential. These capabilities also allowed similar missions far out to sea. The advent of intercontinental bombers, atomic weapons, and missiles provided air power global reach—in the air, on land, and at sea.

In the last half century, Landpower also has moved well beyond the confines of ground operations. Today's armies possess missiles that range the upper reaches of the atmosphere to counter opposing aircraft and to provide ballistic missile defense. Many armies hold significant air power in the form of transport and attack helicopters. The dividing line between close air support of ground operations provided by fixed-wing combat aircraft and helicopters continues to thin. The addition of ground-to-ground missiles of increasing range, precision, and lethality may further reduce air power's role in supporting land warfare.[24] The likelihood of helicopter to helicopter or helicopter to fixed-wing combat aircraft engagement further smudges the dividing line between air and Land-power. Landpower also provides security for air bases, and, historically, Landpower asymmetrically has denied enemy air forces operating bases.[25]

Similarly, land and sea power are interlinked. As the noted British naval theorist, Sir Julian Corbett, stated over 100 years ago, sea power exists predominantly to transport land forces and support land operations.[26] Landpower historically has defeated sea power by seizing enemy harbors and seaports from the land.[27] Conversely, as China's Anti-Access/Area Denial (A2/AD) concept portends, ground-based anti-ship missiles have considerable potential to influence operations far out at sea, especially in the littoral regions. Such influence undoubtedly will increase as technology improves.[28]

The critical issue facing future national leaders and military planners, therefore, is not identifying which element of military power—air, cyberspace, land, sea, or space—will dominate the future security environment. Indeed, such arguments and discussions—usually conducted with intense passion—generate much counterproductive ill will. Rather, in most cases along the conflict spectrum, success will require the application of more than one type of force and power.[29] The key question will be how best to blend the components of military (and usually national) power to provide the desired result.

Figure 2 reflects this broader view of military power and the relationships among air, cyberspace, land, sea, and space power. This notional diagram conveys a number of key concepts. First, as indicated earlier, military power is composed of multiple, subordinate components: air, cyberspace, land, sea, and space. Second, specific force types provide the basis for component power, but they do not automatically equate to power (i.e., land forces are subsumed within but do not equate to Landpower). Third, the intersection of a force type with another component indicates that forces can contribute to other components of military power, as well (e.g., air forces with land or sea power). Cyberspace and space envelop the remaining three inextricably intertwined elements; thus, military power stems from the synergistic and mutually supporting interaction of all five components.

Although not portrayed in the pictograph (for reasons of clarity), the interaction of the other instruments of national power (political, economic, and diplomatic) with the military instrument is equally important for understanding how nations generate and apply power. These instruments could intersect the outer circle of military power, or one or more of the components, depending upon the particular conditions. Nevertheless, the message should be clear: the blending of suitable tools, not an individual instrument, usually leads to success.

In such a notional chart, air or sea power easily could have served as the central point. Moreover, the actual distribution of responsibilities among the forces and components would vary according to the missions, tasks, and desired outcomes. Specific conditions, such as potential opponent, terrain or environment, forces at hand, time available, and the desired national policy objective, also would influence the selection and application of components. In certain cases, one type of force or element of military power might predominate in a particular mission. For example, in conducting Operation FREEDOM FALCON (Libya, 2011), air power—whether land- or sea-based—played the predominant role. Initial operations in Operation ENDURING FREEDOM in Afghanistan, on the other hand, highlighted the close cooperation between air power and Special Operations Forces. Similarly, U.S. Marines launched from air- and sea-based platforms into land-locked Kandahar Province.

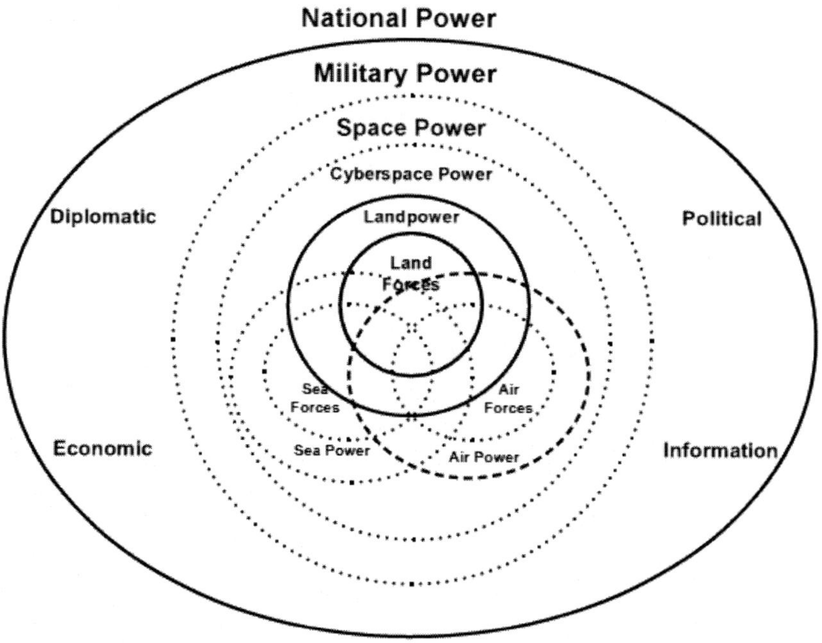

Figure 2. Interdependence.

Initial operations during Operation IRAQI FREEDOM, on the other hand, underscored how the simultaneous integration and synchronization of all elements of military power can generate overwhelming combat power. Once the insurgency broke out after U.S. military toppled Saddam's regime, however, Landpower (to include Special Operations Forces) once again became the primary tool of the U.S. military effort. To be sure, air, cyberspace, sea, and space forces contributed to the fight, but ground forces provided the overwhelming proportion of military power employed.

Despite the interdependence that will characterize most modern military operations, planners must keep in mind that the rising occurrence and significance of interdependent operations does not diminish the importance of any one element of military power. Interdependence will not mean the complete merging of Services or the disappearance of unique forces. There will continue to be missions or tasks that only Soldiers, Marines, airplanes, ships, electrons, or satellites can accomplish. Thus, the drive to interdependence must ensure that the U.S. military retains the requisite unique Service capabilities within the physical domains.

Interdependence also will require national and military leaders to capitalize on the strengths and minimize weaknesses of the individual components. To do so, leaders must first understand the capabilities of each type of military power. They can then determine how best to orchestrate these capabilities to produce desired outcomes, while preventing an adversary from exploiting potential vulnerabilities. In some cases, this may mean that a single component of military power will dominate. In others, it will require the careful orchestration of two or more components to achieve decisive results. In a metaphorical sense, this means having the suitable tools in the toolkit for the problems of the 21st century security environment. For example, when needing pliers, one hopes to find more than screwdrivers and Allen wrenches. Alternatively, one could use a flat tip screwdriver in lieu of a wood chisel, but the results may be much less efficient and effective. At the same time, such use may damage the screwdriver. One could easily extend the metaphor to the idea of having multiple toolkits (components of military power) and being able to draw the most suitable tools from one or more toolkits to address a particular tactical, operational, or strategic level issue.

Specific conditions also will influence force composition. For example, conflict in restricted terrain such as mountains and cities, especially where "collateral damage" is a concern, may limit most activity to land forces. Similarly, within certain smaller-scale contingencies, such as humanitarian assistance, peace support, peace enforcement, or counterinsurgency operations, land forces may have much more utility than air- or sea-based forces, which may be better suited to punish or compel. Equally, air and sea power have areas that will remain their preserve. Control of the air and sea largely (but not solely) will remain the functions of forces that contribute to air and sea power.[30] Unless circumstances or technological developments change dramatically, sea power will continue to provide the means to carry out amphibious operations. Large-scale air transportation will be an air power capability, just as sea transportation undergirds sea power. Cyberspace and space power will undoubtedly contribute. Rarely, however, will either be the primary driver of success.

Notwithstanding the increased interdependence of the elements of military power, policymakers and military practitioners must ensure that they do not take the principle to unnecessary extremes. Once more resorting to an analogy, consider the Leatherman tool. Regardless of size, a Leatherman tool has wonderful utility; however, it also has limitations. It has pliers, but not the best. It has two screwdrivers, but only one size of each type. It has a saw, but no one will cut many two by fours with it.[31]

Nor should leaders pursue interdependent operations simply to ensure that Services get their "piece of the action." As Operation EAGLE CLAW, the failed mission to rescue U.S. hostages held in Iran in 1980, reminds, such provisions can be not simply counterproductive, but catastrophic.[32] Instead, leaders and planners need to implement interdependence carefully to achieve national policy objectives with appropriate efficiency and, more importantly, greatest effectiveness. This will not be easy.

LAND POWER IN THE 21ST CENTURY

Landpower Defined

In 2005, *Field Manual (FM) 1*, *The Army*, promulgated the Army's first official definition of Landpower: "*Landpower* is the ability—by threat, force, or occupation—to promptly gain, sustain, and exploit control over land, resources, and people."[33] Seven years later, *Army Doctrinal Publication 1*, *The Army,* retained the original definition from FM-1, but slightly expanded the explanation of Landpower to include:

- Impose the nation's will on an enemy, by force if necessary.
- Engage to influence, shape, prevent, and deter in any operational environment.
- Establish and maintain a stable environment that sets the conditions for political and economic development.
- Address the consequences of catastrophic events—both natural and man-made—to restore infrastructure and reestablish basic civil services.
- Secure and support bases from which joint forces can influence and dominate the air, land, and maritime domains of an operational environment.[34]

ELEMENTS OF LANDPOWER

Landpower stems from a wide variety of factors. For convenience, these determinants fall into national and military elements that, in aggregate, contribute to Landpower.

National Elements

At the national level, a broad range of factors contributes to Landpower. Historically, for instance, **geo-strategic conditions** have exerted considerable influence over which component would be the most dominant form of military power. Continental powers, such as Russia, Germany, China, India, and France, historically have relied primarily on Landpower.[35] Granted, states or empires with extensive access to the seas (for example, Spain, the Netherlands, and France) sometimes maintained a considerable sea-based force and sought to establish themselves as sea powers, but concern for land warfare and Landpower prevailed overwhelmingly over time.[36] Still, today, most nations rely primarily on ground forces to fulfill their security needs.

Even for the United States, the world's foremost naval power, distinctions over whether the United States is a continental or a maritime power are increasingly irrelevant. The United States has global interests. Because of the diverse geography and geo-strategic conditions of where U.S. national interests lie, the United States will have to possess all components of national military power, to include Landpower. The more pertinent question, therefore, is not which form of military power should predominate, but what proportion of forces and power will most effectively meet the specific conditions of a particular event or crisis.

Economic power obviously has a defining influence on the ability to build and sustain Landpower. This stems not only from the general state of the economy, but extends into how much of that economy is devoted to military power, in general, and Land-power, in particular. The extent of the military and civil industrial base (especially the degree to which the civilian base can easily convert to military use) also will contribute to or detract from Landpower. So too will the ability to generate and sustain technological innovation over time. A country's economic infrastructure, particularly communications, information, transportation, and financial networks, will influence the ability to project Landpower. Finally, as the rise and fall of empires, such as Spain, Britain, Russia, Germany, Japan, and the United

States, amply demonstrates, states must match their economic capacity to meet their security interests or suffer what historian Paul Kennedy termed as "overstretch."[37]

Population and the ability to mobilize that population for economic and military ends also affect Land-power. Obviously, the traditional markers of size, distribution, demographics, class structure, and education will influence the degree of economic power and personnel available for military use. Of increasing importance will be the subset of populace mentally and physically qualified to serve, as well as their propensity to join the Armed Forces.[38]

Lastly, the strategic culture of populations will shape the employment of Landpower. For example, Britain's long seafaring tradition and distrust of standing armies led to a strong navy and small army that relied on allies to assume the major burden of land warfare. Conversely, primarily continental powers, such as France, Germany, and Russia relied heavily on land forces and largely failed as sea powers. Since World War II, the United States has been globally engaged. Whether the United States will sustain that commitment or return to more traditional policies of avoiding foreign entanglements and fielding a small standing army remains to be seen.

The **form of government** affects the nature of Landpower and its employment. Authoritarian political systems, for example, may depend heavily upon Landpower to maintain their regimes. Thus, they pose a threat to their populations as well as to their neighbors. This may result in bifurcated force structures capable of offensive operations against neighbors, as well as gendarmerie or heavily armed security forces for internal control. Conversely, democratic governments may have little or no call to use their military domestically other than for disaster relief or rare and targeted support of civil authorities. Externally, despite the notion that democratic nations have fewer propensities to use military power, democracies will resort to force when their national interests are at stake. In addition, they will structure their forces for offensive and defensive purposes.

The **national will** to use Landpower, particularly in the modern age, has a significant influence on its eventual employment. In sum, the best-manned, equipped, and trained force in the world can be largely irrelevant without the national will to wield that potential; or, at the least, not to oppose its use. The national will to employ Landpower may vary considerably depending upon several factors. First, the nature of national interests involved and the degree of risk to those interests will influence national will. A vital national interest at high risk may make generating national will easier. However, one needs look no further than Britain and France in the Inter-War Era to see that such may not always be the case. Similarly, the current U.S. reluctance post-Iraq and Afghanistan to employ Landpower for less than perceived vital national interests offers another viewpoint. Despite this reluctance, however, many nations, including the United States, appear willing to allow land power to participate in military engagement activities, peacekeeping operations, and humanitarian assistance and disaster relief missions even when vital or important national interests are not at stake.

Military Elements

The core of Landpower obviously stems from the **ground forces** (Army, Marine, and Special Operations Forces; active and reserve components) that are available. Nevertheless, ground forces alone do not represent the full extent of a nation's Landpower. Instead, national and military leaders should think of Land-power in terms of ground forces operating interdependently with the other elements of the U.S. Armed Forces, in coalition with allies and partners, in conjunction with government agencies, and in collaboration with international organizations to promote and protect national interests.

The **institutions** that generate and sustain those forces are equally important to Landpower. In short, the recruiting, training, equipping, maintaining, and sustaining functions that generate and undergird the capabilities of the fighting force are equally essential for creating and sustaining land power. Also important are the doctrinal procedures and systems that create and sustain the common operating culture that allow forces to operate most effectively. Equally critical to an effectively functioning force are the leadership, discipline, and morale that bind the force together. In addition, for a nation with global interests, the ability to project forces to the point of crisis in sufficient time to act effectively and to sustain those forces constitutes a key element of Landpower.

The **human dimension** of military power is nothing new. Indeed, the importance of the human dimension has been well documented since Thucydides wrote his history, *The Peloponnesian War*, nearly 2,400 years ago.[39] Machiavelli and Clausewitz likewise saw the centrality of the human dimension. More modern strategists or historians, such as Colin Gray, Michael Howard, John Keegan, Williamson Murray, and Hew Strachan, have continued to stress the vital importance of the human dimension for understanding war and warfare.[40]

Modern militaries, especially their Landpower components, depend heavily on the ability of innovative, adaptive individuals who can react quickly to rapidly changing conditions. To be successful, land forces must recruit and retain high quality personnel, and train and mold them into cohesive teams. This cohesion stems from individual and collective morale and *esprit de corps* that creates a synergistic whole far greater than the aggregate of individual talents. Without this reservoir of talent, Landpower cannot hope to prevail. Indeed, Landpower, more than the other components of military power, depends upon human interaction and innovation for success.[41] Assuredly, all components of military power rely upon high quality personnel; but there is one key difference. Air and sea forces essentially employ weapons systems or support platforms that require people to operate them. Land forces, conversely, tend to recruit people and then equip them.

One should not confuse the concept of the human dimension with the recently proposed concept of a human domain comparable to air, cyberspace, land, maritime, and space domains.[42] Proponents of establishing a separate and distinct human domain may be unnecessarily muddying the issue. Wars quintessentially are fought between and among humans for control of, or at least influence on, human will. Such control usually (but not always) requires defeat of an opponent's armed forces or control of an adversary's land or population. While air and sea power (and increasingly cyberspace and space power) can temporarily deny control of a particular space or may assist in taking control, they cannot sustain that control on their own.[43] Only Landpower can seize and, importantly, sustain control for a prolonged period. Finally, although some humans live on the sea, some fly in the air, and an increasing number may utilize cyberspace, the fact remains that the overwhelming bulk of humanity occupies the land. Proponents of a separate human domain, therefore, may be making a distinction without a difference that will not withstand scrutiny.

STRATEGIC AND OPERATIONAL VERSATILITY: ROLES AND MISSIONS OF LANDPOWER IN THE 21ST CENTURY[44]

Landpower will continue to have tremendous utility in peace, crisis, and war, and across the conflict spectrum from peaceful competition to general war. Within war, Landpower will continue to apply across all levels of warfare—tactical, operational, and strategic.[45] For these reasons and more (as will become apparent), Landpower will continue to play a critical role in the fundamental purposes of military power: defeat, deter, compel, reassure, shape, and support to the nation.[46]

Defeat

Defeat of an opponent's forces seems a relatively straightforward proposition. As previously indicated, however, defeating an enemy's military is a necessary, but insufficient first step. In some cases, defeat of a country's military forces may be sufficient to control the will of an opponent's leadership. In other cases, defeating an adversary's military forces may not translate into political victory. As the wars in Iraq and Afghanistan reinforce, victory may require bending the will of an adversary's populace, which normally requires prolonged control of those people. While air, cyberspace, sea, and space power can deny control for discrete periods, they cannot sustain long-term physical or psychological control, and in many cases, cyber and space power may be largely irrelevant. Such a level of control usually requires Landpower.[47]

Deter

Deterrence, according to Stanford University professors Gordon A. Craig and Alexander L. George, occurs when a potential adversary concludes that the cost of an action is not worth the potential outcome.[48] For most of history, Landpower provided the overwhelming bulk of deterrent capability. In the latter half of the 20th century, however, air and sea power, especially when augmented with nuclear weapons, added significantly to the calculus of deterrence.

Deterrence in the future, however, may take on a different form than in the recent past and require some changes in the military contribution to that role. The emergence of rogue states, or nonstate actors, with access to nuclear devices or material, but who do not share the long-standing and highly developed culture of deterrence that emerged during the Cold War, may further complicate deterrence. Equally disturbing is the rise of states, transnational organizations, criminal groups, and terrorists that may come into the possession of chemical or biological agents. Because such groups might harbor the perception that there is little likelihood of facing effective retribution, or might be indifferent to such punishment, a threat of nuclear retaliation may not suffice.[49] Moreover, as many states and actors do not possess nuclear weapons, nuclear retaliation would likely appear disproportionate to the world community and, therefore, is unlikely to be credible. Finally, the absence of superpower competition may diminish the heretofore-dominant role of nuclear weapons within deterrence policy.[50]

Conventional forces, therefore, are likely to play a larger deterrent role than in the recent past and the nature of that role may expand. If, for example, a country retains an activist policy of intervening in areas to ensure stability, then the number of potential actors to be deterred may be substantial. Second, the risks posed by potential adversaries will fall across a broader range of the conflict spectrum than was the case with the relatively limited requirements of nuclear deterrence during the Cold War. Third, deterrence depends on communication—messages clearly sent and understood. However, cross-cultural communications, which undoubtedly will increase, can be exceptionally difficult.[51] Because of this rising importance of conventional deterrence, policymakers will have to devote increased attention to designing credible deterrent mechanisms, such as coalitions and alliances, force presence and deployments, and enforced sanctions and embargoes.[52]

Under these cumulative circumstances, Landpower likely will expand its long-standing contribution to deterrence.[53] The fact that many regional powers remain predominantly land powers reinforces this likelihood.[54] This is not to argue for Landpower's dominance in deterrence. Certainly, air and sea power will remain significant contributors to deterrence; however, Landpower has more ability to deter across a wider portion of the conflict spectrum than may be the case with the other components of military power.[55]

Compel

As political scientist and policy practitioner Thomas Schelling noted in 1966, compellence involves the use or threat of force to get an adversary to do what you want.[56] Compellence can range from defeat of an opponent's military forces to punishment to the limited use of force to achieve goals to the threat of force to obtain desired objectives. These latter nuances fall under what Craig and George term coercive diplomacy, where policymakers apply, individually or in concert, the military, diplomatic, and economic instruments of national power to "persuade" another actor to adopt a particular course of action.[57]

Coercive diplomacy is not new; indeed, recorded history offers countless examples. Even in the Cold War, when the risks of escalation to superpower nuclear confrontation tended to circumscribe coercive diplomacy, policymakers had to make difficult choices against the backdrop of the communist threat and the possibility of escalation. The decreased potential for nuclear confrontation, however, may reduce the encumbrances on the use of military power and could lead to coercive diplomacy assuming a larger role in future U.S. policy.[58]

Coercive diplomacy usually demands a blend of the instruments of national power that are context sensitive, are appropriate to achieve the national objectives involved at the lowest possible cost, and are within an acceptable level of risk. Military power, when used as an effectual tool of diplomacy, offers national leaders a broad range of policy options. Landpower, in particular, can respond to low-level conflict, conduct all missions associated with peace operations, participate in smaller-scale contingencies (such as raids, strikes, or limited campaigns), or help prosecute a major theater war. Naturally, the effectiveness of Landpower's contribution will vary with the conditions, as will those of air, cyberspace, sea, and space power. Because Landpower is the principal source of military power for many states and actors, Landpower represents the ultimate form of compellence. The emphasis here is that Landpower uniquely can place an opponent's sovereignty at risk.[59] This combination offers national leaders an extensive set of options for responding to a particular event or crisis.

(Re)Assure[60]

Reassurance, according to historian and strategist Sir Michael Howard, who coined the term, ". . . provides a general sense of security that is not specific to any threat or scenario."[61] The purpose of assurance, however, is not simply to keep allies and friends contented. Assurance serves a country's interests by advancing national values and beliefs; promoting regional stability; improving cooperation among allies, partners, friends, and, occasionally, adversaries; reducing the perceived need for military competition; and cultivating good will. All of these elements (and more) contribute to an improved international security environment that ultimately benefits not only individual nations, but also the global community.

While the presence of air and sea power can assure friends and allies, these partners sometimes may perceive these elements of military power as transient demonstrations of U.S. resolve. In addition, continental nations or regional powers who do not have a long tradition of relying on air or sea power do not necessarily see these elements as an ultimate guarantor.[62] While the importance of the assurance role may have diminished somewhat in the wake of the collapse of the Soviet Union, recent aggressive Russian actions in the Caucasus and, especially, Crimea and Ukraine once more have brought assurance of regional actors and North Atlantic Treaty Organization (NATO) allies to the fore. The dispatch of U.S. land forces to Poland and the Baltic States in response to ongoing Russian aggression once more reinforces that Land-power offers the highest level of national commitment to a partner's sovereignty, offering considerable assurance.

Similarly, recent Chinese activities in East Asia have renewed the importance of assuring U.S. partners and allies in the region. As envisaged in AirSea Battle, air and sea power are likely to play major parts in assurance, but there is a growing recognition that Landpower still has a vital role to play under that concept. Nor have key allies forgotten about U.S. Land-power presence on the Korean Peninsula, or the role of ground forces in the Philippines.[63]

Engagement

The U.S. military also has a significant stake in the peacetime promotion and protection of U.S. national interests and objectives. Over the last 2 decades, the use of the military instrument of power to help shape the international security environment has grown in importance. Generally, shaping activities may include:

- Rotational deployments for exercises and training.
- Foreign attendance in U.S. professional military education activities.
- Building partner capacity.
- Security force assistance.
- Civil affairs support for stabilization, reconstruction, and development efforts.
- Foreign internal defense.
- Counterterrorism and support to counterterrorism.
- Foreign humanitarian assistance and disaster relief.[64]

Additionally, the U.S. Armed Forces can expect increased contributions to the already significant levels of peacetime engagement missions: peacekeeping or other peace operations (e.g., support to diplomacy, peacemaking, peace building, and preventive diplomacy), nation assistance, military-to-military contacts, and security assistance.[65] Indeed, recent history has demonstrated the nature and scope of such support. Humanitarian assistance and disaster relief will no doubt remain critical engagement activities.[66]

While all elements of national military power support engagement activities, Landpower is the most significant contributor. This is not to argue that air and sea power do not participate in engagement activities. U.S. air and sea forces, for example, are key contributors to humanitarian assistance operations. Few civilian organizations in the world or even most militaries have the capability to move massive amounts of supplies as quickly and as effectively to the point of natural or man-made crisis. Equally, air and sea power, individually or in combination with the other components of national military power, help promote stability in key regions of the world through exercises, information sharing, and military-to-military contacts. Air and sea power also provide capabilities needed to prevent or reduce conflicts and threats.

Landpower, nonetheless, still offers the greatest number of options and operational flexibility. Moreover, most current and anticipated partners rely predominantly on land forces for their security. Much of the Middle East, Africa, and Latin America, for instance, have predominantly land-oriented forces and land security issues. In Europe, air, cyberspace, sea, and space power clearly have roles to play, but again, Landpower predominates. Even in parts of Asia, where sea and air forces logically may have a larger role, land forces will still play a considerable part. Thus, Landpower frequently offers policymakers the most suitable instrument of military power.

Support to the Nation

The importance of the critical roles outlined above oftentimes overshadow another vital military role: support to the nation. The U.S. military and, especially the Army, historically have provided considerable domestic support.[67] While the next decades will pose challenges different from the 19th and early 20th centuries, the U.S. military will remain engaged in domestic support operations. Missions could vary from traditional disaster relief and support of civil authorities to combating international crime, drug trafficking, and terrorism; to contributing to border and refugee control; to assisting in the rebuilding of national infrastructure; to responding to ecological disasters; even to supporting the delivery of health care to under-served segments of U.S. society.

Once again, most of these tasks fall to the forces that comprise the basis for Landpower. Other components of military power contribute, but the reality is that the capabilities inherent in air and sea power and the environments in which they operate limit their ability to perform most support roles. Thus, the greatest portion of these missions and tasks fall to land forces, specifically the Army.

Specific Roles and Missions

While a useful starting point, the conceptual underpinnings outlined earlier are only a first step. A necessary second step is to identify more specific roles and missions that U.S. military power, generally, and Landpower, specifically, can expect to perform. Fortunately, a number of key legal, policy, and doctrinal publications establish the most important roles and missions of Landpower. While not exhaustive, the outline that follows offers sufficient extracts from a few key documents that underscore the number, breadth, and scope of missions that U.S. military power, and specifically Landpower, can expect to carry out on behalf of the nation.

At the level of the Department of Defense (DoD), the *Quadrennial Defense Review 2014* established three pillars of U.S. Defense Strategy that influence the roles and missions of Landpower: protect the homeland, build global security, project power and win decisively.[68] In a similar vein, *The National Military Strategy, 2011: Redefining America's Military Leadership* stipulated that the U.S. military and, hence, Landpower, must be able to counter violent extremism, deter and defeat aggression, strengthen international and regional security, and shape the future force.[69]

Key Joint and Service leaders have expanded these general requirements to include more specific missions for the U.S. Armed Forces. For example, in *Strategic Landpower: Winning the Clash of Wills*, General Raymond T. Odierno (Chief of Staff, Army), General James F. Amos (Commandant, USMC), and Admiral William H. McRaven (Commander, U.S. Special Operations Command) have identified the following primary missions of the U.S. Armed Forces:

- Counter Terrorism and Irregular Warfare;
- Deter and Defeat Aggression;
- Project Power Despite Anti-Access Area Denial Challenges;
- Counter Weapons of Mass Destruction;
- Operate Effectively in Cyberspace and Space;
- Maintain a Safe, Secure and Effective Nuclear Deterrent;
- Defend the Homeland and Provide Support to Civil Authorities;
- Provide a Stabilizing Presence;
- Conduct Stability and Counterinsurgency Operations; and,
- Conduct Humanitarian, Disaster Relief, and Other Operations.[70]

For the Army, specifically, 10 U.S. Code 3062 clearly establishes that:

> It is the intent of Congress to provide an Army that is capable, in conjunction with the other armed forces, of:
>
> 1) preserving the peace and security, and providing for the defense, of the United States, the Commonwealths, and possessions, and any areas occupied by the United States;
> 2) supporting the national policies;
> 3) implementing the national objectives; and,
> 4) overcoming any nations responsible for aggressive acts that imperil the peace and security of the United States.[71]

The law further details that the Army ". . . shall be organized, trained, and equipped primarily for *prompt and sustained combat* [emphasis added] incident to operations on land."[72]

Taking into account all of this guidance (and more), *Army Doctrinal Publication* (ADP)-*1*, *The Army*, identifies the current core and enabling competencies for the Army, which also apply more generally to Landpower:

- Core Competencies
  — Combined arms maneuver
  — Wide area security
  — Special operations
- Enabling Competencies
  — Support security cooperation
  — Tailor forces for the combatant commander
  — Conduct entry operations
  — Provide flexible mission command

— Support domestic civil authorities
— Mobilize and integrate the Reserve Components.[73]

The limited guidance outlined here underscores the number and scope of the roles and mission that Landpower (as part of interdependent operations) can expect to perform. Moreover, the events of the last 2 decades have amply demonstrated that these roles and missions are not merely hypothetical. Nor are they likely to be hypothetical in the near term. Granted, some may argue that the future can be different from the past—and perhaps it can be. Recent trends and enduring U.S. national interests argue, however, that Landpower can expect more of the same for the near future.

A key reason behind the reasonable expectation that national leaders will continue to call frequently upon Landpower capabilities is that Landpower offers tremendous utility across almost the entire spectrum of military conflict. (See Figure 3.) As the last 2 decades amply illustrate, Landpower offers significant versatility across the entire spectrum of conflict and throughout the range of military operations. In the last decade, alone, this performance has extended from support to domestic authorities to peacetime engagement activities to shaping the international security environment, to responding to smaller-scale contingencies to joint and combined operations in a two theaters of war.

Highlighting the versatility of Landpower in no way diminishes the utility of the other elements of military power. Cyberspace and space power, however, tend to play complementary rather than individually decisive roles. Air and sea power will remain critical elements for most scenarios and under the right conditions can play decisive individual roles. Indeed, the further to the right on the conflict spectrum, the more effective air and sea power become. However, the further left on the conflict spectrum the generally less effective and, therefore, less appropriate they may be.

Of course, Landpower is not without its limitations. When projected beyond home shores or overseas bases, Landpower depends upon air and sea power for deployment, as well as long-term sustainment and support. Without friendly control of the air and seas, land operations are difficult, if not impossible, to carry out and sustain.[74] When engaged in most smaller-scale contingencies and, certainly, major theater war, Landpower depends heavily upon the capabilities that air and sea power bring to the conflict. Certainly, cyberspace and space power provide critical enabling capabilities.

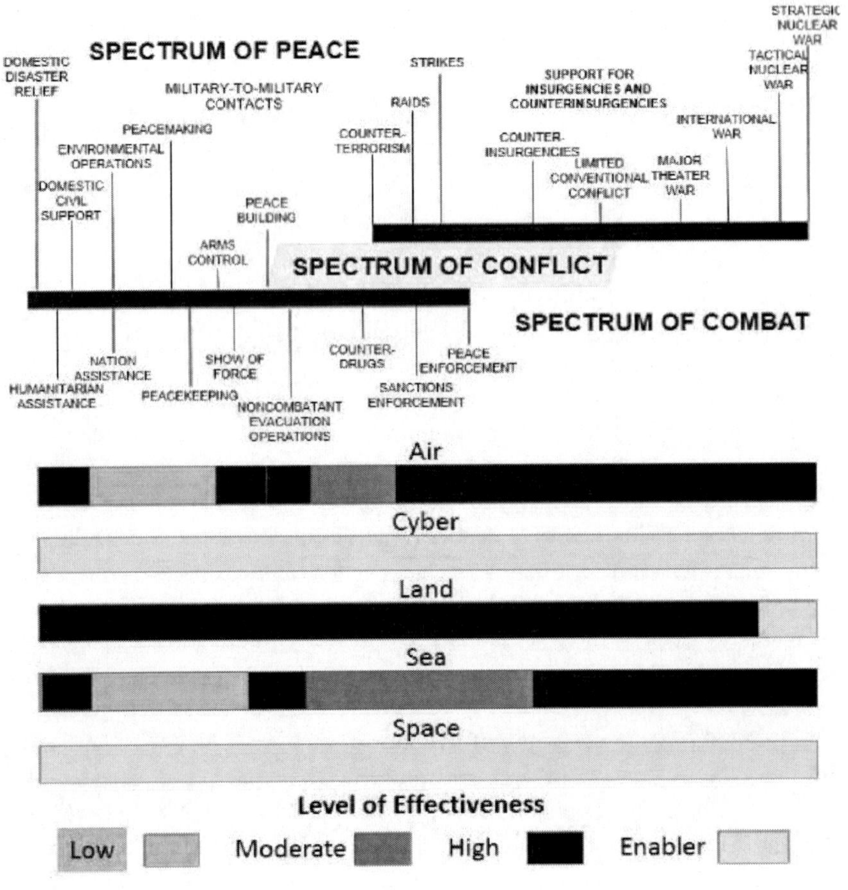

Figure 3. Utility Along the Spectrum of Military Conflict.

Employing ground forces also can present a number of obstacles. First, Landpower may be slower to deploy and may lack the relative ability to strike deep quickly or in as great strength as air and sea power. Second, Landpower also is more prone to friction than the other elements of military power. As analyst Lukas Milevski points out, "Landpower, of all forms of power, has perhaps the greatest density of moving parts; particularly so if one considers all the support it requires to operate effectively."[75] The greater the number of units usually involved in ground operations only compounds these frictions. Weather and terrain also exacerbate these conditions. Additionally, for the near future, opposing land forces have a greater opportunity to disrupt land operations than an adversary's air or sea forces may have to disrupt operations in those domains.[76]

Third, because land forces represent the highest perceived level of U.S. commitment—domestically, as well, as externally—conditions may have to reach crisis proportions before decisionmakers commit Landpower. Such delays may inhibit earlier employment that might have eased circumstances before they erupted in full-blown crisis. Alternatively, deployment of insufficient land forces may encourage an aggressor to act before forces are fully capable of responding. Lastly, if deployed, land forces may be difficult to disengage from active conflicts.[77]

Fourth, an aversion to danger and casualties may inhibit the use of Landpower. Land forces can be the most susceptible to casualties, and the numbers of land forces and their proximity to danger, especially armed opponents, raises the likelihood of casualties.[78] Policymakers, therefore, may view employing Land-power with apprehension. Certainly, since the end of the Cold War, particularly when U.S. ground forces were committed with less than vital national interests at stake, public and political anxiety over U.S. casualties reached significant levels. Whether this trend will continue in the wake of the wars in Iraq and Afghanistan is an open question, but it is possible that such concerns could spill over into crises where important or vital U.S. interests are involved.[79]

In this regard, a perception exists that air and sea power offer a more bloodless—friendly, enemy, or civilian—form of warfare. Part of this perception stems from an American infatuation with technology. Air and sea forces tend to use technologically sophisticated platforms that simultaneously make land forces seem archaic while offering the tempting chimera of weapons that can strike with precision from afar without drawing friendly or too much enemy blood. Compounding the fascination with technology is the manpower intensive nature of Landpower operations that may expose more American sons and daughters to injury and death. Nonetheless, as the supposedly inadvertent Iraqi attack on the USS *Stark* (1987), the Khobar Towers bombing in Saudi Arabia (1996), and the attack on the USS *Cole* (2000) illustrate, sea and air forces also are vulnerable to such casualties.

Finally, land operations oftentimes have much greater media and public transparency than those on the sea and in the air where media reporters and cameras seldom go. Granted, an errant bomb can grab a headline, but most of what happens on the sea or in the air, space, and cyberspace lies beyond the normal reach of media attention. Land operations, however, can come under considerable scrutiny. As a result, if something goes wrong, it is more apparent, more prone to publicity, and more likely to affect U.S. reputation and interests than operations in the other domains.[80]

If recognized, however, these limitations can be offset or ameliorated. In some instances, the other elements of military power can take up the slack or fill in the gaps. Alternatively, leaders and planners may have to recognize the negative aspects and work within them. For example, Landpower holds the potential for higher levels of casualties. As a nation, we need to recognize now that national interests at some future point may cause casualties and build the necessary resilience into the national will. We should not accept the illusion that some other instrument of national military power offers a "clean," casualty free (for the United States, at least) option.

Conclusion: Landpower—A Means to an End, Not an End

An increasingly uncertain and ambiguous international security environment, combined with the complexity of modern warfare, argues for greater clarification of what Landpower means in 21st century terms. These circumstances do not presuppose that the previous essence of Landpower, understood for ages, is no longer relevant. Nothing could be further from the truth, for as the analysis indicates, many of the enduring elements of Landpower remain relevant. Nonetheless, the evolution of Landpower and the growing volatility of the international security environment argue for a more comprehensive understanding of the future roles of Landpower. Equally important, such understanding will assist national leaders in more effectively orchestrating Landpower in concert with the air, cyberspace, sea, and space elements of military power to achieve greater interdependence.

Rarely will such orchestration be easy. Leaders will have to strip away the more extreme or aggressive claims of advocates of a particular component of military power, and identify which capabilities are best suited for a particular task. Because of the dynamic nature of conflict and conditions, such deliberations will be necessary for nearly every new mission. Undoubtedly, jurisdictional quarrels among elements of military power and Services will resurface. While these issues deserve debate, and competitive analysis oftentimes identifies opportunities, key leaders cannot allow such frictions to degenerate into "turf battles" so common over the last half-century.

As a first step in reducing the number, scope, and severity of such turf battles, leaders must not only recognize, but act in accord with, the fact that no one element of military power can provide comprehensive capabilities for every contingency across the entire spectrum. No ground force commander, for example, wants to enter into battle without U.S. air superiority or control of the sea. At the same time, no advocate of Landpower would ever propose that land forces conduct naval operations or seize command of the sea. Yet, air and sea power advocates sometimes propose that they can unilaterally achieve land control.[81]

A better understanding of Landpower that includes strengths and limitations will help policymakers in making future decisions. Only with such a comprehensive understanding will leaders and planners be able to identify not only the capabilities required, but as importantly, from whence those capabilities should come. Absent such understanding, policy and the execution of strategy to implement that policy will suffer.

Landpower's greatest contribution to overall national military power is its inherent versatility. This versatility stems from the types and range of activities Landpower can undertake, and the ability of land forces quickly to adapt existing organizations to meet the demands of a particular mission profile or rapidly changing tactical, operational, or strategic conditions. Landpower capabilities offer national leaders the broadest range of options for handling opportunities or crises. These options cannot be matched by other elements of military power because they are limited by the domains in which they operate or by the nature of their equipment. Landpower's utility is particularly evident along the lower portions of the conflict spectrum. Here, operations rely less on a technological response from a "system of systems" to mass deadly effects and more on human interaction, which Land-power is best suited to supply. This may be especially true for most peacetime engagement and shaping activities.

Not least, the human dimension will continue to dominate war and warfare. Indeed, successful military operations will still rely on the human capacity to react quickly to a highly fluid and nuanced environment to produce decisive results. In counterinsurgency or state-building activities, people usually will be more effective than platform-based solutions.[82] Immersed in the human dimension, Landpower is the most capable component of military power in this most critical of all realms.

A good understanding of Landpower is not an end unto itself. This analysis is only a first step in building an understanding of how to orchestrate land, air, cyberspace, sea, and space power to conduct interdependent operations, where the whole is greater than the sum of the aggregate capabilities of the five elements. In this light, this monograph, therefore, has sought not to exaggerate the capabilities inherent in Landpower or to divide the "military power pie" into better defined, but increasingly irrelevant pieces. Rather, the monograph provides a better understanding of Land-power that will help policymakers place Landpower in its appropriate context, recognize its strengths and acknowledge its weaknesses, while elaborating Landpower's interdependence with the other elements of military power. In this manner, the analysis seeks to facilitate the development of effective policy options and contribute to better decisions, for when considering the employment of military power, such decisions never come easy.

End Notes for Preface

[1] For examples of public opinion following Somalia, see Carolyn J. Logan, "U.S. Public Opinion and the Intervention in Somalia: Lessons for the Future of Military-Humanitarian Interventions," *The Fletcher Forum of World Affairs*, Vol. 20, No. 2, Summer/Fall 1996, available from *dl.tufts.edu/file_assets/ tufts:UP149.001.00040.00013*, accessed June 16, 2014. For public views on the Balkans, see, for instance, Lydia Saad, "Americans Hesitant, as Usual, About U.S. Military Action in Balkans," Gallup News Service, March 24, 1999, available from *www.gallup.com/ poll/3994/americans-hesitant-usual-about-us-military-action-balkans. aspx*, accessed June 16, 2014.

[2] See, e.g., Nathan Freier, "How the Iraq War Crippled U.S. Military Power," *Defense One*, May 1, 2014, available from *www. defenseone.com/ideas/2014/05/how-iraq-war-cr* accessed May 6, 2014. According to a NBC News-*Wall Street Journal* poll, 47 percent of Americans believe the United States should reduce its role in world affairs. Carrie Dann, "47% Say U.S. Should Reduce Role in World Affairs," available from *www.nbcnews.com/#/politics/f* accessed May 12, 2014. As Nathan Freier *et al.*, point out, war costs, national debt, and a belief that large-scale wars are no longer likely exacerbates this war weariness. See Nathan Freier *et al.*, U.S. *Ground Capabilities through 2020*, A Report of the CSIS New Defenses Project, Washington, DC: Center for Strategic and International Studies, October 2011, p. vi. For a realist perspective on recent events, see Steven M. Walt, "No Hawks Here," *Foreign Policy*, April 17, 2014, available from *www.foreignpolicy.com /articles/2014/04/17/no_hawks_here_realists_international_relations_war_peace* accessed April 17, 2014. It is important to note, that even in the wake of Vietnam, the United States helped engage in counterinsurgency operations in Latin America.

[3] See, as examples, *National Security Strategy of the United States*, Washington, DC: The White House, May 2010, p. 2; Tyrone C. Marshall, "Debt is Biggest Threat to Security, Chairman Says," American Forces Press Service, September 22, 2011, available from *www.defense.gov/news/newsarticle.aspx?id=65432,* accessed June 16, 2104; and *Defense Budget Priorities and Choices*, Washington, DC: Department of Defense, January 2012.

End Notes for Chapter

[1] Carl von Clausewitz, *On War*, Michael Howard and Peter Paret, eds. and trans., Princeton, NJ: Princeton University Press, 1984, p. 593.

[2] *Army Doctrine Publication* (ADP)-*1*, *The Army*, Washington, DC: Headquarters, Department of the Army, September 2012, p. 1-4, available from *armypubs.army.mil/doctrine/ DR_pubs /dr_a/pdf/ adp1.pdf*, accessed March 1, 2014.

[3] The official term used by the U.S. Army War College is Landpower (initial capitalization, one word).

[4] Just as national power consists of the diplomatic, informational, military, and economic elements, each sub-component has constituent parts. For the purposes of this analysis, military power will consist of air, cyberspace, land, sea, and space power. In this monograph, an element of national (or military, etc.) power is something that contributes to aggregate national (or military, etc.) power. An instrument of national (or military, etc.) power is a mechanism through which national leaders wield some portion of that accumulated national (or military, etc.) power. The terms elements(s) and component(s) are synonyms.

[5] That said, sea power played the dominant role in exploration and colonization over several centuries.

[6] See Alfred Thayer Mahan, *The Influence of Sea Power Upon History, 1660-1783*; and Sir Julian Corbett, *Some Principles of Maritime Strategy*, both contained in David Jablonsky, ed., *Roots of Strategy*, Book 4, Mechanicsburg, PA: Stackpole Books, 1999. Internet accessible versions of Mahan and Corbett may be found at Project Gutenberg, *www.gutenberg.org/ebooks/13529* and *www. gutenberg.org/ebooks/15076,* respectively, accessed June 7, 2014.

[7] Giulio Douhet, *The Command of the Air*; and William Mitchell, *Winged Defense: The Development and Possibilities of Modern Air Power—Economic and Military*, are in Jablonsky, *Roots of Strategy*. For a concise overview of interwar air power theory, see David MacIsaac, "Voices from the Central Blue: Theorists of Air Power," in Peter Paret, ed., *Makers of Modern Strategy from Machiavelli to the Nuclear Age*, Princeton, NJ: Princeton University Press, 1986, pp. 624-647.

[8] Martin Libicki, a leading cyberspace expert, argues that the time may not yet be ripe for a cyberspace prophet. See Martin C. Libicki, "Why Cyber War Will Not and Should Not Have a Grand Strategist," *Strategic Studies Quarterly*, Vol. 8, No. 1, Spring 2014, pp. 23-39.

[9] ADP 1, p. 1-4; *Joint Publication* (JP) *1-02*, *The Department of Defense Dictionary of Military and Associated Terms* (hereafter JP 1-02), available from *www.dtic.mil/doctrine /new_pubs/jp1_02.pdf,* accessed March 1, 2014, does not define Landpower. Nor does JP 1-02 define air power or sea power. JP 1-02 does define "land control operations: The employment of ground forces, supported by maritime and air forces (as appropriate) to control vital areas of the land domain. Such operations are conducted to establish local military superiority land operational areas." *Ibid*., p. 159. Interestingly, JP 1-02 also defines sea control operations ("The employment of forces to destroy enemy naval forces, suppress enemy sea commerce, protect vital sea lanes, and establish local military superiority in vital sea areas." *Ibid*., p. 240), but does not define air control operations.

[10] General Raymond T. Odierno, General James F. Amos, and Admiral William H. McRaven, *Strategic Landpower: Winning the Clash of Wills*, n.d., p. 1, available from *www.tradoc.army.mil/ FrontPageContent/Docs/Strategic%20Landpower%20White%20Pa-*

per.pdf, accessed March 1, 2014. The scope of the Strategic Land-power Task Force's charter reinforces this conclusion. The task force is to:

- address the role of forces "that operate on land," and how they can contribute to preventing and containing conflict;
- address why past tactical and operational successes have not always achieved strategic outcomes;
- reinforce the necessity of integrating our understanding of achieving physical objectives with a fuller understanding of, and consideration for identifying and achieving human objectives in the formulation and execution of strategy, operational plans, and tactical actions; and,
- expand the dialogue around the "social sciences" of warfare alongside the "physical sciences" of warfare.

[11] JP *1, Doctrine for the Armed Forces of the United States,* Washington, DC: Government Printing Office, March 25, 2013, p. I-1, available from *www.dtic.mil/doctrine/new_pubs/jp1.pdf,* accessed March 3, 2014. See John Spanier and Robert L. Wentzel, *Games Nations Play*, 9th Ed., Washington, DC: Congressional Quarterly Inc., 1996, pp. 293-384, for a discussion of these instruments and their employment.

[12] Figure taken from JP- *3.0, Joint Operations*, August 11, 2011, p. V-1, available from *www.dtic.mil/doctrine/new_pubs/jp3_0.pdf,* accessed March 1, 2014.

[13] In compliance with the U.S. Army War College policy of nonattribution, this speaker must remain anonymous. For a broader discussion of this issue, see Colin S. Gray, *Defense Planning for National Security: Navigation Aids for the Mystery Tour*, Carlisle, PA: Strategic Studies Institute, U.S. Army War College Press, March 2014.

[14] Micah Zenko, "100% Right 0% of the Time," *Foreign Policy*, October 16, 2012, available from *www.foreignpolicy.com/ articles/2012/10/16/why_the_military_cant_predict_the_next_war*, accessed February 24, 2014. Nor is Secretary Gates alone in this regard, as key military leaders such as former Chairman, Joint Chiefs of Staff Admiral (Ret.) Mike Mullen, and former Central Command Commander General (Ret.) James Mattis have offered similar evaluations of our forecasting abilities. *Ibid.*

[15] Michael Howard, "Military Science in an Age of Peace," *Journal of the Royal United Services Institute*, Vol. 119, No. 2, March 1974, p. 7.

[16] Nassim Taleb, *The Black Swan: The Impact of the Highly Improbable*, New York: Random House, 2007.

[17] JP 1-02 defines the space environment as "The environment corresponding to the space domain, where electromagnetic radiation, charged particles, and electric and magnetic fields are the dominant physical influences, and that encompasses the earth's ionosphere and magnetosphere, interplanetary space, and the solar atmosphere," p. 251.

[18] JP 1-02 defines cyberspace as "A global domain within the information environment consisting of the interdependent network of information technology infrastructures and resident data, including the Internet, telecommunications networks, computer systems, and embedded processors and controllers," p. 67.

[19] William T. Johnsen, *Redefining Land Power for the 21st Century*, Carlisle, PA: Strategic Studies Institute, U.S. Army War College, 1998, p. 16. For a slightly different view of the interaction among the Services, see Colonel John Bonin, "Mutually Supporting Relationships," Exercise Joint Warrior, Discussion Issue 6, Interrelationships Land-Sea-Air Forces, April 1, 1998.

[20] JP 1-02, "joint operations—a general term to describe military actions conducted by joint forces and those Service forces employed in specified command relationships with each other, which of themselves, do not establish joint forces," p. 152.

[21] JP 1, p. I-2.

[22] The idea of Globally Integrated Operations contained in the *Capstone Concept of Joint Operations* (CCJO) addresses aspects of the concept, but not in sufficient detail. *Capstone Concept for Joint Operations: Joint Force 2020*, Washington, DC: Joint Staff, September 10, 2012, pp. 4-13, available from *capstone.dodlive.mil/ files/2013/04/CCJO-Sep2012.pdf*, accessed March 27, 2014.

[23] Where general air parity existed, e.g., throughout World War I, the ability of aircraft to observe offensive preparations allowed opponents to mass defensive forces, thereby contributing to the stalemate that marked most of the Western Front.

[24] For instance, the PAC-3 version of the Patriot Air Defense Missile System and the Army Tactical Missile System (ATACMS) equipped with Brilliant Antiarmor Submunitions (BAT) and Sense and Destroy Armor (SADARM) munitions.

[25] The obvious examples are the Allied campaigns in North Africa, Italy, and Europe and the U.S. island-hopping campaigns in the Pacific during World War II. I am indebted to my colleagues, Professor John Bonin and Professor Leonard Fullenkamp, for this observation.

[26] Sir Julian Corbett, *Some Principles of Maritime Strategy*, David Jablonsky, ed., *Roots of Strategy* Book 4, Mechanicsburg, PA: Stackpole Books, 1999, pp. 170-171. Also see Sir Julian Corbett, *Some Principles of Maritime Strategy*, Part I, Chap. 1, New York: Longmans, Green, and Co., 1911, p. 1, available from *www.gutenberg.org/files/15076-h/15076-j.htm,* accessed June 10, 2013.

[27] See, e.g., J. Michael Robertson, "Sea Control Remains Critical," *Proceedings*, April 1997, p. 80. There is a long history of such operations: from the Peloponnesian Wars, to Alexander the Great versus the Persians, to Napoleon denying Britain bases in the Mediterranean and Baltic Seas, to Union forces capturing Confederate seaports in the U.S. Civil War, to the land capture of German submarine pens in World War II. Once again, I thank Professor John Bonin for bringing these citations to my attention.

[28] These capabilities are not just quantitatively different from the past, where shore batteries could deny ships access to ports and a relatively narrow band of coastline. Today, land- or air-launched cruise missiles extend their reach hundreds (and soon, perhaps, thousands) of kilometers out to sea. This represents a significant qualitative change in the land-sea power equation.

[29] As an example of an argument against the likelihood of success using a single defeat mechanism, see the critique of the Douhetian defeat mechanism in AirSea Battle, in Huba Wass de Czege, "Improving the Mental Maps that Inform Defense Policy," *Army*, February 2014, p. 20.

[30] For example, Army air defense and missile defense systems will contribute to air power and land-based anti-missile systems will influence the employment of sea power.

[31] I am grateful to Lieutenant Colonel Darry Grossnickle, USMC, for prompting this analogy.

[32] For an account of the operation, see Admiral James Holloway *et al.*, Rescue Mission Report, August 1980, available from *www.history* accessed April 26, 2014.

[33] *Field Manual* (FM) *1, The Army*, Washington, DC: June 2005, p. 1-1. For a discussion of various ways to define power prior to the Army's official efforts, see Johnsen, *Redefining Land Power for the 21st Century;* H. Richard Yarger, "Land Power: Looking Toward the Future through a Green Lens," *Strategic Review*, Winter 1999, pp. 22-30; and Michael

Evans, *The Continental School of Strategy: The Past, Present, and Future of Landpower*, Duntroon, Australia: Land Warfare Studies Center, 2004.

34 ADP 1, p. 1-4.

35 For an excellent exposition on the qualities of the "Continental School," see Evans, *The Continental School of Strategy*.

36 Interestingly, Spain, Japan, and the United States also have generated considerable Landpower. Britain and The Netherlands offer, perhaps, the best example of heavy reliance on sea power, followed by the United States in the late-19th and 20th centuries. For a critique of Britain's reliance on sea power at the expense of Landpower, see Russell F. Weigley, *The Age of Battles: The Quest for Decisive Warfare from Breitenfeld to Waterloo*, Bloomington, IN: University of Indiana Press, 1991, pp. 88, 162-163, 321, 338-339, 449, 539-540. (I am indebted to Professor John Bonin for bringing this information to my attention.) Granted, continental powers occasionally struck out to sea (e.g., France in the 17th and 18th centuries, and Germany in the early-20th century), but their strategies and operations focused almost entirely on Landpower.

37 See Paul Kennedy, *The Rise and Fall of the Great Powers: Economic Change and Military Conflict from 1500 to 2000,* New York: Random House, 1987.

38 For examples of recruiting concerns, see Major General Allen W. Batschelet, Rick Ayer, and Colonel Mike Runey, "The Army We Need; the Army We Can Have," *Army*, February 2014, pp. 30-32, available from *www.ausa.org/publications/armymagazine/archive/2014/Documents/02February/Batschelet_February2014.pdf*, accessed June 9, 2014.

39 Robert B. Strassler, ed., *The Landmark Thucydides: A Comprehensive Guide to the Peloponnesian War,* New York: Touchstone Books, 1996.

40 The human dimension so pervades the works of these scholars that specific citations are not useful.

41 The U.S. Army's Human Dimension Concept, for example:

> . . . provides a framework for how the future Army must select, develop, sustain, and transition Soldiers and Army Civilians to prevent, shape, and win in the 21st century. This concept redefines the parameters of the human dimension as encompassing the cognitive, physical, and social components. It includes all aspects of Soldier, Civilian, leader, and organizational development and performance essential to raise, prepare, and employ the Army in unified land operations.

U.S. Training and Doctrine Command (TRADOC) Pamphlet 525-3-7, The U.S. Army Human Dimension Concept, May 21, 2014, p. 5, available from *www.tradoc.army.mil/tpubs/pams/TP525-3-7.pdf*, accessed June 7, 2014.

42 For a brief overview of the concept of the human domain, see, for example, Claudette Roulo, Armed Forces Press Service, "McRaven: Success in Human Domain Fundamental to Special Ops," June 5, 2013, available from *www.defense.gov/news/news-article.aspx?id=120219,* accessed June 7, 2014; and Otto Kreisher, "Landpower Leaders Stress Need to Understand Human Domain in Warfare," Association of the United States Army, Annual Meeting 2013, available from *www.ausa.org/meetings/2013/Annual-Meeting/Pages/story42.aspx,* accessed June 7, 2014. For a broad discussion of the concept, see Frank Hoffman and Michael C. Davies, "Joint Force 2020 and the Human Domain: Time for a New Conceptual Framework?" *Small Wars Journal*, June 10, 2013, available from *smallwarsjournal.com/jrnl/art/joint-force-* accessed June 7, 2014.

43 Lukas Milevski, "*Fortisisimus Inter Pares*: The Utility of Landpower in Grand Strategy," *Parameters*, Summer 2012, pp. 7-8.

[44] "Roles are the broad and enduring purposes for which the Services and U. S. Special Operations Command were established by law." "Core Mission Areas are broad DoD military activities required to achieve strategic objectives of the *National Defense Strategy* and *National Military Strategy*," and "Functions are the appropriate or assigned duties, responsibilities, missions, or tasks of an individual, office, or organization as defined in the National Security Act of 1947, including responsibilities of the Armed Forces as amended." The term "function" includes purpose, powers, and duties. Specific Functions of the Services and U.S. Special Operations Command are located in DoD Directives. Robert M. Gates, *Quadrennial Roles and Missions Review Report*, January 2009, pp. 3-4, available from *www.defense.gov/news/jan2009/qrmfinalreport_v26jan.pdf*, accessed April 26, 2014.

[45] There may be little utility, therefore, in defining Land-power against a specific level of warfare. Thus, defining "strategic landpower" as does the Strategic Landpower Task Force (SLTF, *Clash of Wills*, p. 3) or describing strategic land power as an "operational concept" (Gary Sheftick, "Strategic Landpower Doctrine must be developed, involve new skills," *AUSA News*, March 2014, p. 20) may be counterproductive. Such formulations could limit how national leaders perceive the utility of Landpower across the spectrum of conflict, artificially limiting the scope of its contribution to national objectives and interests.

[46] See, for example, Thomas C. Schelling, *Arms and Influence,* New Haven, CN: Yale University Press, 1966, p. 1-34; and John F. Troxell, "Military Power and the Use of Force," J. Boone Bartholomees, Jr., ed., *U.S. Army War College Guide to National Security Strategy,* 5th Ed., Carlisle, PA: Strategic Studies Institute, U.S. Army War College, 2012, pp. 224-225.

[47] As Milevski has pointed out: "The potential to take and actually exercise control is the core difference between Landpower and all other tools, military and nonmilitary, of grand strategy." Milevski extended his argument, noting that, "Landpower, because it alone has the capability to take and then exercise control on the decisive geography of war, is the unique tool capable of and necessary for imposing one's will on the enemy directly and actively." Milevski, "*Fortissimus Inter Pares*," p. 14.

[48] Gordon A. Craig and Alexander L. George, *Force and Statecraft: Diplomatic Problems of Our Time*, New York: Oxford University Press, 1983, p. 172. For an excellent discussion of this concept, see *ibid.*, pp. 172-188.

[49] The difficulty of tracing exactly those responsible for an isolated or terrorist act is well known. Equally, zealots of ideological or religious ilk may be indifferent to any potential retribution.

[50] The United States must retain a credible nuclear deterrent. Long-standing concepts will retain utility, albeit with greatly reduced numbers of warheads and delivery systems.

[51] Steven Metz, "Deterring Conflict Short of War," *Strategic Review*, Vol. 22, No. 4, Fall 1994, pp. 44-51.

[52] Deterrence theory existed long before the advent of nuclear weapons, but conventional deterrence theory has been overshadowed the last 60 years by nuclear weapons. John J. Mearsheimer, *Conventional Deterrence*, Ithaca, NY: Cornell University Press, 1983, regenerated interest in the topic. For discussions of more recent renewed interest in conventional deterrence, see e.g., Michael S. Gerson, "Conventional Deterrence in the Second Nuclear Age," *Parameters*, Vol. XXIX, Autumn 2009, pp. 32- 48; and Tom Nichols, "The Case for Conventional Deterrence," *The National Interest,* November 12, 2013, available from *national interest.org/commentary/the-case-conventional-deterrence-9381,* acces- sed June 9, 2014.

[53] For a discussion of the reasons behind this trend, see William T. Johnsen, *The Future Roles of U.S. Military Power and Their Implications*, Carlisle, PA: Strategic Studies Institute, U.S. Army War College, April 18, 1997, pp. 7-8.

[54] The origin of the Korean War offers a more modern example of the deterrent effect of Landpower from the perspective of an opponent. North Korean Dictator Kim Il Jung and Soviet leader Joseph Stalin were reluctant to take overt action against South Korea until U.S. ground troops withdrew. The withdrawal occurred in late-1949, and the invasion followed in June 1950. See William Stueck, *The Korean War: An International History*, Princeton, NJ: Princeton University Press, 1995, p. 31.

[55] For example, the Dwight Eisenhower and John Kennedy administrations discovery that "massive retaliation" using nuclear weapons delivered by air-and sea-based platforms was not always a credible deterrent across the conflict spectrum led to the emergence of the doctrine of "flexible response" that offered national leaders more policy options.

[56] See Schelling, *Arms and Influence*, pp. 69-92. Deterrence and compellence differ in that deterrence seeks to dissuade an actor from undertaking a particular action, while compellence seeks to "persuade" an actor to do what you want.

[57] For a discussion of coercive diplomacy, see Craig and George, *Force and Statecraft*, pp. 189-203. Examples might include economic sanctions or embargoes, demarches, military raids, or punitive campaigns.

[58] Events of the post-Cold War Era lend credence to this conclusion. One could view the invasions of Afghanistan and Iraq as examples of where initial use of coercive diplomacy failed, thereby requiring campaigns to overthrow the governing regimes. Russian actions in the Caucasus and Ukraine also are pertinent examples. Demands for U.S. action in Syria and international efforts to constrain Iran's nuclear ambitions are also examples.

[59] I am grateful to Colonel Tarn Warren for this insight.

[60] "American English" tends to use the term "assure" versus "British English" that tends to use "reassure." This is another example of two great peoples separated by a common language, but as Sir Michael Howard coined the original term, a tip of the hat in his direction.

[61] Sir Michael Howard, "Lessons of the Cold War," *Survival*, Vol. 36, No. 4, Winter 1994-1995, p. 165.

[62] As my colleague, Professor Leonard J. Fullenkamp, aptly points out: "What made Pax Britannica credible was not just the great English Navy, although it was important. What made England great was the certainty that on the heels of crisis came the 'thin red line' of British troops that would make good on England's promises." See also Captain Paul Lushenko, "The Real Question Isn't Naval Presence but How to Best Empower U.S. Partners in Asia," *The Best Defense, Foreign Policy*, available from *ricks.foreignpolicy.com/posts/2014/04/09/the_real_question_isnt_naval_presence_but_how_to_best_empower_us_partners_in_asia*, accessed April 9, 2014.

[63] For a description of AirSea Battle, see DoD, Air-Sea Battle: Service Collaboration to Address Anti-Access & Area Denial Challenges, May 2013, available from *www.defense.gov/pubs/ASBConceptImplementation-Summary-May-2013.pdf*, accessed June 9, 2014. For an example of reassurance to countries in the region, see, for example, President Barack Obama's trip to Japan, South Korea, Malaysia, and the Philippines in April 2014 that culminated with the signing of a new U.S.-Philippines defense pact. Thomas Maresca, "Obama Visits Philippines; U.S. Announces Defense Pact," *USA Today*, April 27, 2014, available from *www. usatoday.com/story/news/world/2014/04/27/us-philippines-defensepact/8299491/*, accessed June 9, 2014.

[64] Secretary of the Army John M. McHugh and General Raymond T. Odierno, *2012 Army Strategic Planning Guidance,* Washington, DC April 19, 2012, p. 5.

[65] In this period of increasing turmoil and instability, conflicts such as Libya, Syria, Mali, Central African Republic, Nigeria, and many other possible candidates seem more likely to occur. While some might argue that the United States should avoid such operations, U.S. national interests or the interests of our close allies and partners may draw us into such conflicts.

[66] Militaries generally possess the capabilities needed for rapid and effective response to natural or man-made disaster, or providing capabilities beyond those available to a host nation. This may take the form of humanitarian assistance (such as the response to the earthquake in Haiti in 2010 or the tsunamis that struck Indonesia and Thailand in 2004 or Fukushima, Japan in 2011) or humanitarian intervention in the Balkans from 1991 to 1999.

[67] For example, exploring the western frontier, serving as a constabulary force in newly settled regions, engineering railroads and inland waterways, constructing the Panama Canal, and conducting medical research.

[68] Barak Obama, *National Security Strategy, 2010,* Washington, DC: The White House, available from *www.whitehouse.gov/ sites/default/files/rss_viewer/national_security_strategy.pdf,* accessed April 26, 2014; Admiral M. G. Mullen, *The National Military Strategy of the United States of America, 2011,* Washington, DC: DoD, available from *www.army.mil/info/references/docs/NMS%20 FEB%202011.pdf,* accessed April 26, 2014; Leon Panetta, *Defense Budget Priorities and Choices*, Washington, DC: DoD, January 2012, available from *www.defense.gov/news/Defense_Budget_Priorities.pdf,* accessed April 26, 2014; and Chuck Hagel, *Quadrennial Defense Review 2014,* Washington, DC: DoD, pp. 13-22, available from *www.defense.gov/pubs/2014_Quadrennial_Defense_Review.pdf,* accessed April 26, 2014.

[69] *The National Military Strategy (NMS) of the United States of America: Redefining America's Military Leadership*" 2011, p. 4. The NMS further called for a Joint Force that is:

- Adaptable and capable of deterring aggression and providing a stabilizing presence, especially in the highest priority areas and missions in the Asia-Pacific region and the Middle East, while still ensuring our ability to maintain our defense commitments to Europe and other allies and partners.
- Ready, rapidly deployable, and expeditionary such that it can project power on arrival.
- Capable of defending the homeland and providing support to civil authorities.
- Possessing cutting-edge capabilities that exploit our technological, joint, and networked advantage.
- Able to reconstitute quickly or grow capabilities as needed.
- Above all, manned and led by the highest quality professionals.

See also *Defense Budget Priorities and Choices*, p. 1.

[70] *Strategic Landpower*, p. 2. Also outlined in ADP-1, p. 3-1.

[71] 10 USC 3062, Washington, DC: Government Printing Office, available from *www.gpo.gov/fdsys/pkg/USCODE-2011-title10/ html/USCODE-2011-title10-subtitleB-partI-chap307-sec3062.htm*, accessed April 25, 2014.

[72] *Ibid.*

[73] ADP-1, p. 3-3-3-8. For some proposed changes to these core competencies, see Major Jeremy Sauer, Chris Stolz, and Captain Michael Kaiser, "Core Competencies for an Army of Preparation," *Army*, February 2014, pp. 40-45.

[74] The obvious case is where an opponent possesses air power capabilities. Even when an adversary has little or no air forces or power, friendly air power routinely makes critical contributions to the land battle: close air support, interdictions, and strategic attack.

[75] Milesvski, "*Primus Inter Pares*," p. 13.

[76] *Ibid.*, p. 12. For example, many countries possess little or no modern capability in sea or air forces and no capability in space forces.

[77] On the inability to disengage, see Nathan Freier, "MIA in QDR: A Unifying Vision for Land Forces," *Small Wars Journa*l, 2010, p. 3, available from *www.smallwarsjournal.com/,* accessed on February 16, 2014.

[78] Milevski, "*Primus Inter Pares*," pp. 12-13.

[79] Political and public concerns over U.S. intervention in Libya and Syria are illustrative.

[80] I am grateful to Dr. William Pierce of the U.S. Army War College for bringing this thought to my attention.

[81] See, e.g., the more extreme claims of air power advocates in the wake of the bombing campaign in Kosovo, initial operations in Afghanistan, or the "shock and awe" air campaign early in the Iraq War.

[82] For example, people are more effective than laser guided bombs at separating and then developing effective working relations between formerly warring parties.

In: Landpower in the 21st Century
Editor: Elizabeth Baker ISBN: 978-1-63483-172-7

Chapter 2

ALWAYS STRATEGIC: JOINTLY ESSENTIAL LANDPOWER*

Colin S. Gray

FOREWORD

The strategic quality of Landpower is widely known, but not widely understood. In this monograph, Dr. Colin S. Gray explores and explains the meaning of strategic Landpower. He is concerned particularly to argue that, although Landpower today must function in a joint environment, typically it is the dominant element in the team for U.S. national security.

The monograph lays emphasis upon the place of the human domain that leads in the role played by ground forces in strategy. Because of some widespread conceptual misuse, many people are not used to thinking of Landpower as a strategic instrument for American security policy. Dr. Gray aspires to help reduce the popularity of this important misconception. It is necessary for good policy that American Land-power should be considered and debated properly, which is to say in appropriate strategic terms.

DOUGLAS C. LOVELACE, JR.
Director, Strategic Studies Institute and U.S. Army War College Press

---

* This is an edited, reformatted and augmented version of a monograph issued by the Strategic Studies Institute, February 2015.

About the Author

COLIN S. GRAY is Professor of International Politics and Strategic Studies at the University of Reading, England. He worked at the International Institute for Strategic Studies in London, United Kingdom (UK), and at the Hudson Institute in Croton-on-Hudson, NY, before founding the National Institute for Public Policy, a defense-oriented think tank in the Washington, DC, area. Dr. Gray served for 5 years in the Ronald Reagan administration on the President's General Advisory Committee on Arms Control and Disarmament. A dual citizen of the United States and UK, he has served as an adviser to both the U.S. and British governments. His government work has included studies of nuclear strategy, arms control, maritime strategy, space strategy, and special forces. Dr. Gray has written 27 books, including *The Sheriff: America's Defense of the New World Order* (University Press of Kentucky, 2004); *Another Bloody Century: Future Warfare* (Weidenfeld and Nicolson, 2005); *Strategy and History: Essays on Theory and Practice* (Routledge, 2006); *Fighting Talk: Forty Maxims on War, Peace and Strategy* (Potomac Books, 2009); *National Security Dilemmas: Challenges and Opportunities* (Potomac Books, 2009); *The Strategy Bridge: Theory for Practice* (Oxford University Press, 2010); *War, Peace and International Relations: An Introduction to Strategic History*, 2nd Ed. (Routledge, 2011); *Airpower for Strategic Effect* (Air University Press, 2012); *Perspectives on Strategy* (Oxford University Press [OUP] 2013), which is the follow-on to *Strategy Bridge*. The final volume in the Strategy Bridge trilogy, entitled *Strategy and Defence Planning: Meeting the Challenge of Uncertainty*, was published by OUP in 2014. Dr. Gray is a graduate of the Universities of Manchester and Oxford.

Summary

American Landpower is a strategic instrument of state policy and needs to be considered as such. The purpose of this monograph is to explore and explain the nature of Landpower, both in general terms and also with particular regard to the American case. Five themes drive through this work. Specifically, it is argued that: (1) Landpower is unique in the character of the quality it brings to the American joint team for national security; (2) the United States has a permanent need for the human quality in Landpower that this element provides inherently; (3) Landpower is always and indeed necessarily strategic in its meaning and implications—it is a quintessentially strategic instrument of state policy and politics; (4) strategic Landpower is unavoidably and beneficially joint in its functioning, and this simply is so much the contemporary character of American strategic Landpower that we should consider jointness integral to its permanent nature; and, (5) notwithstanding the nuclear context since 1945, Landpower retained, indeed retains, most of the strategic utility it has possessed through all of history: this is a prudent judgment resting empirically on the evidence of 70 years' experience.

In short, the strategic Landpower maintained today can safely be assumed to be necessary for security long into the future. No matter how familiar the concept of strategic Landpower is when identified and expressed thus, it is a physical and psychological reality that has persisted to strategic effect through all of the strategic history to which we have access.

* * *

As we relearned in Afghanistan and Iraq, the United States should not enter a conflict with a strategic plan that amounts to little more than engaging and destroying the enemy order of battle. Lasting strategic success is not a function of enemy units eliminated or targets destroyed. A successful strategic outcome rests, as it has since time immemorial, on winning the contest of wills.

General Raymond T. Odierno, USA,
General James F. Amos, USMC, and
Admiral William H. McRaven, USN [1]

As this nation goes forward into a new century one thing remains certain; Landpower will remain central to our strategic success. There is no more unmistakable or unambiguous display of American resolve than the highly visible deployment of Landpower.

General Raymond T. Odierno, USA,
General James F. Amos, USMC, and
Admiral William H. McRaven, USN[2]

Land operations have a uniquely significant role, in both peacetime and conflict, in addressing human factors. This assertion arises from the recognition that: 1) the Army, Marine Corps, and Special Operations Forces significantly contribute to the activities central to influencing the "human domain" short of war, such as peacekeeping, comprehensive military engagement, security force assistance, building partner capacity, and stability operations; 2) in conflict, the same forces are those most intimately and closely involved with the human networks—friendly, enemy, and neutral—that comprise the "human domain," and 3) strategic success most often occurs within the land domain, especially in the shared space between humans and the land, and potentially in the shared space between humans and the cyberspace domain.

General Raymond T. Odierno, USA,
General James F. Amos, USMC, and
Admiral William H. McRaven, USN[3]

STRATEGIC LANDPOWER HISTORICAL CONTEXT

Geography is not joint, but warfare has become ever more noticeably so over the course of the past century. That said, even conceded, the idea of Land-power should be clear enough, although it assuredly is not beyond all frontier types of conceptual challenge. My subject is neither confused nor should it be at all confusing, unless, that is, one chooses to make it so. Although there are libraries crammed with studies of warfare on land, writings addressed explicitly and more or less discretely to exploration and explanation of Landpower are not in abundant supply. One explanation for thinness in the literature simply is that few gifted scholars have felt moved to explain what they believe is already common knowledge because it is or ought to be obvious. Landpower is both an empirically verifiable reality and also a conceptual construction. The need for reliable joint cooperative military effort renders the idea of Landpower apparently vulnerable to some erosion of the right to exclusive ownership and command. The constructivist categorization that may seem able to divide up the world into distinctive geographical domains can appear troublingly vulnerable to the political, strategic, and budgetary consequences of technological innovation. When one geographical domain cannot effectively resist functionally enabling assistance from capabilities designed primarily to exploit other geographies, understandably and predictably interservice rivalries are fostered and may fester. Common sense tends to be an early casualty in the politics of interdomainal military procurement and influence. This monograph has no wish to add fuel to any conflagration enabled by the military, for strategic nonexclusivity in Army competence and authority.

This discussion of strategic Landpower cannot avoid the necessity of identifying a true partnership of the "both and" kind. To be specific, Landpower is both essential for American national security and yet must depend critically upon the strategically enabling potential of other military domains. The somewhat uncomfortable dualism just expressed is generically all too familiar in a subject such as this that appears to make a mockery of distinctive hierarchy in relationships. For the reasons argued subsequently, Landpower unquestionably must be regarded as the premier category of military capability, but several caveats require recognition as potentially substantial hazards to the safety of the logic of the Landpower case. One notable contemporary reason why Landpower lacks sovereign strategic authority is because its effectiveness in deterrence or in combat action could be negated were the United States to be obliged to resort to large-scale nuclear use with a similarly nuclear armed enemy. It is true to claim that one might endeavor to define strategic Landpower in a way so highly permissive as to include the means of nuclear bombardment. However, a bid for such inclusivity in favor of Landpower plainly would not be culturally consistent with now traditional American habits of mind and organization concurring military categorization.[4] Russians may well view their long-range nuclear-tipped and land-based missile forces essentially as artillery, but Americans do not and are unlikely to follow suit. However, strange to say, perhaps, the obvious potential menace posed by nuclear weapons to any verdict on combat by conventional Landpower does not serve greatly to demote the relative significance of the Army. It is necessary to appreciate the significance of commonsense boundaries to strategic argument. The case for strategic premiership that is the Army's does not need to rest upon implausible, or worse, arguments claiming an ability to wage any or all combat of any character. To be assessed as critically important, there is no need for Landpower to make implausible acquisitive grabs in a hunt for the ability to cope sufficiently well with any and all categories of challenge.[5]

It is important to recognize that the high concept of strategic Landpower is essential both for what it includes and what it does not. Indeed, the integrity of the concept and the category of capability and implied behavior to which it refers, require clear enough boundaries if they are to function usefully.

Although seapower, airpower, and now cyberpower, plainly can be regarded not unfairly as strategic categories that inherently are variably competitive with Landpower, also their legitimate distinctiveness is essential for the generic-like distinctiveness of Landpower. Indeed, given the cumulative accretion of military capabilities with domainal ancestry other than of a landward nature, it is vitally necessary for the conceptual and practical organizational integrity of Landpower that the frontiers demarcating seapower and airpower, for examples, are maintained meaningfully.[6]

The validity of the concept of Landpower is evidenced convincingly by facts "in the field." Although Landpower is a conceptual construction, it does have historically verifiable empirical markers. Most empires are troubled by some residual persisting uncertainty over the proper frontier of their domains. It is only sensible to recognize that Landpower is a concept that can be interpreted in a way uncomfortably permissive of opportunistic seizure by military organizations whose primary focus is not the land. In truth, historical circumstance, military and strategic culture, and even individual personality, can play a role in the determination of what is and what is not regarded locally as Landpower.

For reasons readily attributable largely to their geography and historical experience, particularly as those potent sources of influence are mediated by culture, many countries have never been in serious danger of being uncertain about the relative seniority granted officially and popularly to their geographically distinctive armed forces. For particularly clear examples, Britain has long regarded its Royal Navy as the Senior Service, while Russia and Germany have never been in serious peril of misunderstanding the ever arguably "luxury" nature of their episodically impressive naval power.[7] Monarchical and then Imperial France periodically was proved persuadable that its greatness both required and could secure preeminence at sea as well as on land, but typically that belief, or one should say hope, was not well enough founded. The strategic frontier of France was on or about the Rhine, which had to mean that strategic Landpower needed to be the core of concern for French statecraft and strategy. Britain learned in the 17th century to distrust Landpower in the form of a standing army, which meant that it could make a virtue of the strategic necessity of its insularity for the achievement and sustenance of maritime preponderance.

The American case has been a mixed one that tracks recognizably with the broad influences of national geography and historical circumstance mentioned earlier. Although American Landpower, inclusively understood, was episodically briefly and deeply impressive in the early-1860s and the late-

1910s for obvious reasons of wartime mobilization, there is no doubt that it cannot properly be assessed as being even somewhat equal in national cultural esteem to the military power and systems of Prussia/Germany and Russia. The physical and political geography of America prior to the construction of the Panama Canal in 1914, and the transoceanic immigrant origins of many Americans, meant rather ironically that the truly continental scale of the mature national geography was more than marginally offset in popular appreciation by the practical difficulty of transcontinental mobility. The relatively high national security that geographical insularity on a continental scale provided came naturally at a notable and politically contestable strategic price. Obviously enough, while American Landpower could and periodically did trouble Canadian and Mexican neighbors in North America, continental insularity also meant that the United States lacked easy access to the principal areas of world contention in and about Eurasia.[8] In short, when the United States decided that it should intervene strategically in a forceful manner in world affairs, it found that command of the sea (and forward bases) across oceanic distances to Europe (and Africa) and Asia was absolutely essential. In addition, in the 1940s, the aerial domain also needed to be commanded before American Landpower could be brought into contact with the enemies of the day.

Contrary to appearances, perhaps, it is not my intention here to challenge the core ideas expressed so clearly by Generals Raymond Odierno and James Amos and Admiral William McRaven in the epigraphs to this monograph. Rather, I seek to emphasize the distinctiveness, indeed the uniqueness, of the American strategic historical experience. American Landpower has been no less strategic than were German and Russian/Soviet Landpower, but its historical manifestation was nationally different, albeit not conceptually in kind. The strategic meaning of Landpower is the same among states, but geography and history provide individual national contexts for strategic meaning.

THE CONCEPT OF STRATEGIC LANDPOWER

At present, the Army chooses to define Landpower as "the ability—by threat, force, or occupation—to gain, sustain, and exploit control over land, resources, and people."[9] There is much to recommend in this definition, given its privileging of the idea of control. An admirable vigor pervades the definition, while there is also room for some discretion on the boundary. It may be noticed that, although Landpower is discussed widely almost as a team player alongside other categories of power differentiated by geography or function, there is a sense in which it should be regarded as a *primus inter pares* (first among equals). The Army is not confused about this, but alignment in a common categorization as power, albeit duly modified to fit particular geography (e.g., seapower and airpower), can encourage misunderstanding. If anything, the very concept of Landpower, which unavoidably and indeed necessarily, privileges physical geography, somewhat undermines appreciation of its own full and true case. There is some danger of the Army, Marine Corps, and Special Operations Forces inadvertently diminishing the weight of their argument as a consequence of their combined effort to promote Landpower. The official definition quoted at the beginning of this section is good in that its non-specificity regarding military means allows for useful inclusion of a wide discretion. Nonetheless, as a consequence of the broad geographical categorization, there does remain a somewhat inappropriate implicit commonality. In other words, Landpower appears to be regarded as another geographically identified category, more than marginally comparable to the sea and the air. Landpower risks under appreciation because of the comparability with the sea, air, and now cyber as well, that appears to be suggested by its name as an adjectival modifier of the concept of power.

It has been my first-hand experience for nearly 50 years as a teacher and author on strategy, that it can be challenging to accord Landpower the quality of recognition it merits, because so often it is presented in the historical and conceptual company of other apparently more than marginally like ideas, such as seapower, airpower, and cyberpower. For obvious, and indeed all but self-evident reasons with admirably joint connection, it can be difficult for the Landpower triad of Army, Marine Corps, and Special Forces to be frank, yet also fair as well as honest.

What needs to be gripped and grasped beyond room for argument is the permanent geographical fact which is an enduring practical reality for strategy— that the land matters most for humans. Indeed, we have no geographical choice. The other geographical environments, including the constructed ones now composed of cyberspace, and the functionally awesome domain of nuclear weapons, can be important, occasionally indeed even conclusively so. But the consequences of threat and action in all geographical contexts ultimately must have strategic and political meaning for and on land. This is hardly news, but exciting analyses pertaining to actual and potential conflict at sea, in the air, in cyberspace, and even concerning the political efforts of nuclear threat, all, finally and determinatively, have meaning for the land and Landpower. This is a matter of nature, but it is a fundamental truth of our human condition that can be hard to find if the distinctive geographies of our whole context are not appreciated correctly.

To claim that the land always matters most because it is the only physical geography that we can inhabit is not to claim, save in a formal sense, that all human conflict must be decided as a direct consequence of happenings on land. However, given that we humans can organize our security only for where we are able to live, on land, it has to follow that extraterritorial behavior needs translation as to its meaning for the strategic narrative on land. In common with physical geography, strategic history inherently is more than joint; it is a unified, at least a collective, whole, albeit sometimes confusing and untidy, as well as incomplete.[10] Strategic history may well appear to repeat itself in parallel narratives, even if, more likely when, the paths of causation contributing to events are notably different. Overall, however, strategic threat, anxiety, and action, no matter the particular military forms taken at the time, have to be expressed recognizably in political and strategic terms readily explicable with reference to an inclusive understanding of Landpower.

I have argued elsewhere that the most potent question in the methodological arsenal of the strategist is the challenging, and sometimes even offensive appearing, demand for understanding carried by the elementary query, "So what?"[11] Given that we can only inhabit and politically organize the land, it must follow that all strategic behavior judged relevant to our situation has to bear upon our Landpower, certainly as this concept currently is officially defined.

The Army's (et al.) definition of Landpower is a permissive one, particularly given the broad inclusivity allowed by the focus upon a desired consequence of American behavior—control. Since it is an eternal truth that we cannot inhabit nonterritorial geography, it has to be the case that military forces of all kinds ultimately can be challenged by the basic, deceptively simple seeming, question deployed earlier. Whether or not ground forces are heavily involved, the single strategic historical narrative that is our human estate should be understandable as Landpower. The other geographical environments may well be militarily, strategically, and then consequentially politically, episodically more important than U.S. land—as in ground—power. But, the single and unified narrative of American strategic history must show effect in or for Landpower. Properly comprehended, as in intelligent understanding of the currently official definition of Landpower, there is no strict requirement for strategic Landpower to be delivered by ground forces. The geopolitical and therefore also the geostrategic context for American international behavior is nearly always about the acquisition of influence at a transoceanic distance. It follows that there can be no doubting the strategic necessity for substantial supporting, and occasionally even substitutional, effort on the part of military agents other than ground forces. Strategic Landpower must be a heavily and diversely joint enterprise. U.S. ground forces always require military cover and other kinds of support from friendly air assets, much of which in transportation and bombardment roles will need to be of medium and long range. Similarly, the absolute necessity for aerial support is paralleled by the necessity of transoceanic logistic provision, which for purposes other than brief raids still has to be transported by sea.

The core of the strategic argument for the U.S. Army, Marine Corps, and Special Operations Forces is borne by the powerful concept of control.[12] These forces, though primarily the Army, inherently have qualities with high potential strategic value unique and indispensable to the nation. These qualities should be well known, but still there is a plausible case to be made for emphasizing their extraordinary relative importance. It is necessary to differentiate between general and contextually particular truths. Bearing in mind that we are investigating and explaining two heavily interconnected, but nonetheless distinctive, ideas—American strategic Landpower on the one hand, and American ground forces on the other—it soon becomes quite apparent why this vital distinction is simultaneously both important yet ultimately rather trivial in strategic and ultimately political assessment. What follows is a shortlist of ideas that serve to capture most of what needs to be caught in the particular conceptual web that is the prime focus of this monograph.

Some Pre-Theory on Strategic Landpower

1. The case for the strategic relevance of Landpower must vary enormously with the scale and particular character of each individual conflict. Also, given that the character of future conflict is not reliably predictable, the United States requires of its Landpower that it should be ready enough for overseas deployment on relatively short notice. Obviously, the scale of the problem(s) must largely determine the lead-time required to ready forces for deployment that may have to be of protracted duration.

2. The unpredictability of policy demand for actions by Landpower, and the variety of possible geopolitical and geostrategic contexts, mean that the American approach to strategic Landpower needs to be considerably inclusive. The immediate roles required to be played by U.S. ground forces may be

modest. Indeed, it is probable that in many cases the bare fact of their commitment and deployment may well be more significant strategically and politically than is their anticipated tactical effectiveness.

3. "Boots on the ground" carry, or at least imply, a quality of American desire or demand for political control of behavior locally that cannot credibly and effectively be borne by other kinds of military power. Air and missile power certainly can achieve control, indeed, the entire theory, policy, and strategy of nuclear deterrence rests on this belief. However, the quality of behavioral control that ground forces can secure is unique. The presence of those forces carry a message of reassurance or of potentially coercive menace that may be up close and even personal.

Also, the local deployment of ground forces typically requires a quality of local social and cultural engagement that can be strategically vital for American understanding; such engagement cannot be achieved from altitude or at sea. Needless to say, the potential benefits of a Landpower—as ground power—commitment have to be assessed in balance with its distinctive hazards. However, the danger and cost involved in being strangers in a strange land, foreigners amid an alien culture, today are quite well understood.[13] Nonetheless, it remains true to say that there is a quality of political and even cultural commitment inherent in the forward deployment of American ground forces that is not, and cannot be, replicated by other kinds of action, almost regardless of the relative strength in their strategic promise. It must be said that many of the tough lessons learned in Iraq and Afghanistan are likely to age and perish in the 2010s, now that counterinsurgency (COIN) has lost its political, strategic, and military attractions for a while that may last for 10 or 20 years. Although COIN certainly is, indeed ought to be, the most engaging of contact behavior in the human domain, it does not follow that our recent protracted COIN experience should be regarded definitively as the field test for the strategic utility of American Landpower.

4. It should never be forgotten that strategic force is military force considered and assessed for its political consequences. Awesome and possibly shocking though destruction may be when delivered from a considerable distance, one is bound to say that U.S. Navy Rear Admiral J. C. Wylie was definitely persuasive when he wrote:

> The ultimate determinant in war is the man on the scene with the gun. This man is the final power in war. He is Control. He determines who wins. There are those who would dispute this as an absolute, but it is my belief that while other means may critically

> influence war today, after whatever devastation and destruction may be inflicted on an enemy, if the strategist is forced to strive for final and ultimate control, he must establish, or must present as an inevitable prospect, a man on the scene with a gun. This is the soldier.[14]

Wylie's advice is not a magical elixir for ensuring that military success will be succeeded by strategic benefit. Not infrequently, people forget that strategic history is always flowing in a great stream of time, and that military victory or advantage may not result in the benign political effect that one might carelessly assume to be authoritative.[15] The point needing emphasis here, properly assisted by the wise Rear Admiral, is that strategic effect has to be measured in its, political consequences. The reason why this must be so is because it is only policy, expressing political wishes, that can justify and legitimize the threat or use of strategic Landpower. The nexus between policy and strategy often is considerably closer than some scholars and many citizens assume to be the case. The austere basic elements of the theory of strategy that usually is taught in institutions of higher military education, typically distinguish clearly between strategy's military ways and its political purposes.[16] But, frequently in practice this can prove to be a notionally clear distinction that is not allowed to provide much by way of helpful guidance over practice.[17] Plainly, the potent and attractively inclusive concept of strategic Land-power requires considerable care in its handling, since it brushes, at the very least, against the policy/politics "box" in a PowerPoint slide. This troubling thought now must be considered critically and rigorously if we are to be confident that the conceptual dimension to this analysis does not pose a lethal menace that cannot be overcome at tolerable cost to the authority that should be allowed to the idea of strategic Landpower.

It is perhaps ironic that such an almost self-evidently useful concept as strategic Landpower should be as vulnerable to ill-considered doubt as it is. This may be a case not unlike that made for genius in war, to the effect that unquestionably extraordinary talent in command tends to be balanced more than somewhat by unattractive personal characteristics. The concept of strategic Landpower has high merit both as theory and in its practical implications. But, there is trouble both with the modifying and defining adjective and with the noun itself. The fact that this trouble is not well founded does not suffice to cancel criticism. In part, the criticism is avoidable, but also in quite good part, it refers to professional matters that are largely discretionary and therefore inherently more than marginally political in an inclusive sense. I need to be unambiguous as to the meaning of leading concepts and descriptors. Most especially, there is a necessity for clarity of meaning, as well as proper use, of principal terms. To those ends, I will explain the meaning of strategic and of Landpower. Many expert defense professionals may well differ from me on my explanations: so be it.

Strategic

Strategic, the adjective, is misused very widely in its attribution to particular kinds of military forces because of their inherent nature or their presumed potential significance. This is simply wrong. Indeed, it is more than just wrong because it is a conceptual error that has harmful consequences for defense and war planning. In truth and pragmatically, all military forces, be they great or small in number and assignments, are latently, residually, strategic. Strategy is not effected by inherently strategic acts, but rather by the consequences of tactical and operational level behavior. Those consequences must vary hugely in relative (consequentially strategic) weight from situation to situation. To designate some kinds of forces clearly either as strategic or tactical is a cardinal error in military theory; the fact that states have made this mistake for several generations now does not miraculously expunge the error. Strategy is all about the consequences of tactical behavior. It should not be particularly difficult to understand why it is crucially important to the quality in policy for the military instrument and its behavior to be assessable in terms of the consequences of its actions. If one confuses the intended doing of strategy with tactical practice, then it will not be surprising if one is lost in a no-man's land of confusion. What one would be saying would be that there are strategic, as contrasted with tactical, objectives (or targets, or forces). Strategic does not mean inherently nuclear, long-range, or even exceptionally important.

The fact that the "strategic" adjective is so profusely, and indeed officially misused, does not somehow render it correct, or even just right enough. To summarize pointedly, the U.S. Army, by proper definition, inherently is a strategic instrument. By this, I mean that its potential and actual behavior must have influence, great or small upon the course of strategic history. The Army does not have some strategic, as may be differentiated from tactical, tasks, because that distinction is logically and practicably erroneous. This essential point was made most clearly by Dr. Antulio Echevarria when he explained that "all events in war have weight; even the least can have disproportionate effects."[18] Strategy consists of the consequences of tactical behavior. There are no lesser "tactical" duties. In order to grasp fully the meaning and implications of this elementary binary distinction, all that one needs do is to simplify the challenge as being in essence a distinction between cause and consequence. I appreciate that, when the tactical behavior in question appears very slight in the total context and narrative of national military effort, it will be difficult to accept as legitimate the idea that the modest scale of action under consideration nonetheless has some slight strategic meaning. The concept of strategic Landpower is intellectually healthy when it can be regarded as a philosophical and theoretical step in the right direction, though I must confess to being dismayed by the apparent need for the redundancy, since Landpower cannot possibly be other than strategic in its potential, let alone in practice.

Landpower

Strategy can be problematic both in its design and in its practice when the politics that contribute massively to policy function to create effectively a collectivity of effort toward national security. Landpower can be rendered conceptually and then practicably uncertain for reason of an erosion of distinctiveness. I am troubled about the official definition of Land-power by analogy with the same reason that a thoroughly welcoming ecumenical approach to religion has the potential to dilute the core of what I may believe to be the truth. There is not a real problem here over the integrity of this concept of Landpower, but the Army should scarcely need to be advisedly prudent concerning the need to accommodate potentially contributing agents from other sovereign domains of strategic endeavor. It is appropriate to recognize and welcome jointly helpful assistance to the Army's predominant Landpower on the part of the navy, air, space, and cyber—not to mention significantly the contribution by way of intrawar deterrence that nuclear armed forces may supply. But it is likely to be deemed important that the most formally licensed contributors to American Landpower should not imperil their military strategic leadership position. It can be challenging to discuss this aspect of the subject because authentically unified strategic argument about what is best for national security can hardly help but be brushed with some of the less wholesome features of inter- and even intraservice politics. Of course, it is only natural for contenders to play hard in support of their home team, but that team may be a geographically distinctive armed service, or a functionally separate element thereof, as contrasted with an entire national strategic effort.

In principle, the Landpower concept is not eroded and possibly diluted by high inclusivity of definition. However, Landpower in practice, which most essentially has to mean land control, can be vulnerable to actual as well as potential weakening by diffusion, as the control function is performed by military agents less committed to the core task of land and population control.[19] It is advisable that a state's army should be reluctant to shed many arguably specialist tasks as a consequence of political pressure, let alone joint good will. One needs to be cautious in explaining the reasons for such restraint in enthusiasm for joint endeavor. Fundamentally, the reason is because of the strong advisability of prudence in performance of the core Landpower mission. The essence of Landpower duty is control of a particular land area, territory, and what is on it for as long as policy requires. To fulfill this mission, protracted engagement may be necessary, possibly entailing some co-existence, if not necessarily cooperation, with a local population whose political sympathies and leanings cannot be assumed always to be friendly.

It should not be forgotten that what makes Land-power strategic are the consequences of its behavior. There are many diverse ways in which a state can attempt to secure political influence where it most matters in the hearts, but probably more reliably in the minds of adversaries or those currently politically uncommitted. But, undoubtedly there is a uniquely persuasive (and coercive) quality to the local presence of the man on "the scene with the gun," to employ Wylie's telling phrase yet again. It is important that Americans should resist strategic capture by what can be made to appear as attractive alternatives to strategic Landpower. The leading attractions of most relevance here are budgetary economy and a greater prudence in political commitment. In other words, it is usual for there to be several alternative strategic ways in which political ends might be sought. It is important to recognize that the historical contextual reality almost always seems compatible with at least a shortlist of possibly appropriate alternative strategic approaches. That said, perhaps conceded, it is scarcely less significant for American policy to understand fully the nature of strategic Landpower and the reasons for that nature.

Strategic Landpower at its core comprises the ground combat forces of the state. In theory at least, recognition of strategic jointness should not confuse or mislead. What matters most for the discussion here is that the geo-strategically unique context of war, certainly of conflict, should be fully and accurately understood. No matter how great or small may need to be the assistance to, and support of, American land combat forces by other forces at and from the sea, the air, in space, and in cyberspace, such help will be needed. It is my contention that Landpower with the tactical character of forces built and trained to conduct ground warfare in its several forms must remain and be regarded authoritatively as essential. What is unique about military Landpower is its ability to persist in contested territory in the quest for control. Of course, the measure of control sought over adversarial behavior may not always be attainable at a cost the American political system finds tolerable, given the contemporary definition of national interest. But, the case for strategic Landpower cannot rest upon confident expectation of prudence in the policy that American politics determines.

The "strategic" in the concept of strategic Land-power must rest in practice on the quality of values and assessments that are made. However, there is and can be nothing in the strategic Landpower concept itself that guarantees against misuse or even just bad luck. The value of this concept lies most essentially in its direction of attention to the overarching mission of control of land and what and who is on it. If the concept of strategic Landpower is deemed unduly inclusive, too permissive of assistance by ancillary military (*et al.*) agents other than ground combat and combat support forces, then it may be necessary to substitute a more exclusive official understanding of Landpower for the current one. Attractive though it certainly is in its corralling of any and all sources of influence over happenings on the ground, there is little doubt that the concept in probable effect comprises a charter for possible dilution of effort. When interpreted with good will, intelligently regarding the occasional peril in ill-conceived or clumsily executed "jointery," there is no significant cause for alarm. However, conceptual formulae with unpoliced frontiers are likely to promote interservice and interfunctional strife that would be strategically unhelpful. Today's concept of strategic Landpower is vitally important to the Army, Marine Corps, and Special Forces, but it could benefit from some enhanced clarity as to the unique strategic purpose of military Landpower.

WHY STRATEGIC LANDPOWER IS UNIQUE? WHAT IS DIFFERENT ABOUT IT?

In order to understand fully Landpower, it is essential to grasp what is unique about it. Indeed, the differences in nature, not only in character, from other geographically distinguishable domains should be so obvious as to be in little need of identification, let alone emphasis here. Nonetheless, there is a shortage of full and proper appreciation of Landpower relative to military power designed to function in and from the other geographies.

I will make a modest effort to explain just why Landpower is and has to be of prime strategic importance. However, the argument here would be defeated in grisly strategic practice were nuclear deterrence to suffer a brief lapse at the wrong moment in super and great power relations. There is an extremely potent and persuasive case to be made on behalf of Land-power, but it does have limits. Unless one were to attempt to accept an extreme liberality of inclusiveness, it is neither relevant nor helpful to attempt to stretch conceptually the Landpower domain so as to render it as embracing nuclear-armed forces of intercontinental range. In other words, although Landpower would be a vitally significant participant in any conflict process that might be concluded with nuclear warfare conducted on a large scale, once a substantial nuclear "exchange" was either imminent or actually extant in process, Landpower most likely would lose relative significance. Indeed, it may not be an exaggeration to argue that the bilateral conduct of nuclear warfare on a large scale probably would render the prosecution of further strategic efforts problematic in the extreme. If this is granted as a strong probability, the strategic quality of Landpower could well prove of little importance. Large-scale nuclear employment certainly is a relevant concern for theorists (and practitioners) of strategic Landpower, but it is one that need not, and hence should not, hinder progress in this analysis. I choose not to allow the hopefully distant possibility of a large scale American nuclear exchange either with Russia or China to obstruct the path toward proper understanding of strategic Landpower. It is sufficient for our purpose here simply to note the grim but most likely rather distant prospect of nuclear warfare and move on. This is a classic "What if . . ." of future strategic history that cannot be permitted to control and thereby shape our understanding of today and tomorrow. What follows in this section is written unavoidably in the knowledge of nuclear possibilities, but such happenings are judged to reside in the mercifully bare short list of game-changing possibilities that ought not to detain attention further in this monograph.

The question of greatest moment for analysis and explanation here is the one posed in the title to this section: rephrased a little from the section title, we must ask "What is different about strategic Land- power; how and why is it unique?"

The Land Matters Most

We are a species able to live only upon the land. This means that all our cultural, economic, political, and strategic business has to be conducted with territorial reference and context. Even global maritime trade makes sense only with reference to its territorial origins and destination. Maritime logistics are essential to globalization, but that is solely a transportation narrative; the demand and the supply both require territorial definition. It is all too commonplace for writers today to be so bedazzled by contemporary diversity in logistics, and by the sheer variety of adaptive geographical exploitation expressed in military arsenals, that the enduring most senior significance of territoriality appears to be lost. The character of commerce and of warfare is ever changing, but we have been, and must remain, land animals. It has to follow that political organizations and their military agents must understand security concerns and anxieties ultimately and unavoidably in territorial terms; and those terms always need relation to safety in and of the political home, the homeland, which is a most telling concept in its implications.

Landpower Is About Proximity for Control

From time to time, the United States asks more of its armed forces than the securing of some influence over foreign decisionmaking. In addition, what is required is a physical control that possibly, indeed probably, will have to be achieved coercively. It is relatively rare for us to need the ability to control behavior in this nonpermissive way, but it does occur. There are threats as well as actual violent behavior that must be opposed, stopped, and even punished. While plainly hostile behavior certainly can be harassed and possibly halted by a wide variety of measures, the quality of control achievable by the "man on the scene with the gun" has a definitive quality unmatchable by other agencies. This is not to suggest that the local presence of Landpower itself can resolve political problems that may also be significantly cultural, but the local and potentially enduring presence of our soldiers assuredly alters the local context within which new decisions by foreign agencies will have to be made.

The virtual occupation of foreign lands by means of menace (and more) from altitude, or from over the horizon at sea, is not the strategic or moral equivalent to the occupation, if necessary the seizure, of foreign territory, and presence in the closest of proximity to foreign nationals. The down-side to the proximity and human contact achieved by a Landpower presence is too obvious to need much comment here. Obviously, it can be difficult in the extreme for the United States to distinguish between a local presence and possibly military (and policing for public order) effort that is sufficient, and one that is too much. It is a problem endemic in warfare that, notwithstanding rather naively optimistic theory and policy that was authoritative through most of the 1960s, competitive effort in a violent conflict cannot be controlled predictably and reliably. At least this is true if we are determined to prevail strategically and politically.[20]

In summation, the dynamics of a conflict can begin to take the lead over policy and its politics, meaning that the former will serve the latter, rather than vice versa, as should be the case. Plainly, the high potential strategic value of a local deployment of American Landpower is likely to stimulate—for a while, at least—greater effort on the part of local opposition. What is certain is that the forward deployment of this Landpower will raise the political stakes significantly for an administration with American voters (and parents and other loved ones). This high quality of personal political commitment will be both of almost inestimable positive value for the quality of American political commitment, but also inevitably will comprise a major creation of policy-political vulnerability. All countries care more about the safety of their own soldiers than they do about casualties among foreigners, including allies. This is inevitable and indeed usually quite proper. It is exactly the very quality of care felt by Americans about the forward deployment into probable military action of their soldiers that renders strategic Landpower so potent a commitment, stamped though it is, and indeed should be, with acute policy concerns on the domestic front.[21]

Strategic Landpower and the Importance of the Human Domain

The grand concept of strategic Landpower can appear so elevated and abstract that it appears to resist understanding in human terms. General Charles Krulak, U.S. Marine Corps, went some way, possibly even too far, toward proper appreciation of the individual human contribution to great enterprises of state with his idea of the "strategic corporal."[22] To many commentators, this concept seemed extravagant: after all, what could be the strategic meaning of behavior by a corporal? Surely strategy was discussed and decided by people of high rank. In fact, as noted already in this monograph, corporals do strategy—they have some strategic effect whether or not they are aware of it at the time or even in some retrospect. Although strategy certainly is designed, decided, and implemented as direction at a high level of command, as, if not more, important is the fact that strategy actually is done in the only zone of behavior possible, which is the tactical. Strategy bereft of tactics and operations essentially is meaningless aspiration. Strategy and its strategist author conceive and plan what will be attempted, and it may well be sensible to extend the idea of strategy so as to include command.[23] However, the strategist as conceptualizer, planner, and commander is envisaging the consequences of his adversarial direction of tactical and operational performances. The entire process that results in strategically significant behavior is inherently and essentially human. Landpower really is about soldiers. They are supported and enabled to be effective by particular technologies and logistics, but they do not "serve" equipment, rather the equipment serves them. The technical performance of machinery is of the highest relative importance to military professionals who must perform their duty at sea, in the air, and in cyberspace. The landward domain, in contrast, finds military equipment both essential and important, but not usually critically so.

The key reason why the land domain is unique and different is because so much of significance that occurs on it is subject to human discretion. A critically important enabler of this human discretion is the rich variety of geography—human and natural—and the wide scope of possibilities that render thought and behavior difficult to predict, given the pertinent opportunities and hindrances. Of course, there are moral qualities common in importance across domains; courage, determination, fortitude, integrity, honesty, and so forth. However, the geo-physics of the domains other than the land that require extremes of dependence upon the competitive quality of technology (e.g., ships, aircraft, and computers), routinely need to ask less of the military personnel committed to their use and exploitation than do the forces that express and perform as strategic Landpower. The abstraction that is the concept of Landpower always descends in practice to the behavior of people in uniform, no matter how technologically advanced their equipment.

The historical record shows that troops require armament good enough or sufficiently adaptable to meet the demands of their tactical and operational requirements. Superior technology may be exploited in order to secure tactical advantage, but only rarely is a technical lead in weaponry the most plausible reason explaining satisfactorily military success in battle. For example, American success in its deployment and employment of Landpower in both the world wars of the 20th century owed relatively little to technological advantage. To understand what happened strategically in 1918 and then in 1944-

45, one needs to look a long way beyond, and behind, the quality of rival equipment in widespread American use.[24] In land warfare, sheer quantity (of many kinds) can have a quality all its own. Also, decisions as to how weapons will be used, and the highly variable facts concerning the measure of human determination that soldiers will choose to show under extreme pressure, must fuel uncertainty over relative adversarial performance. Accepting the risk of overstatement, one should endorse the quite common assumption that performance in war depends more upon the ways in which weapons are used than upon the competitive combat quality of the weapons themselves—within reason, I must hasten to add, because this can be a dangerous idea to endorse uncritically and too readily. To lay emphasis, as we should, upon the superior significance of the human terrain that is the core of Landpower is not to suggest or even imply that dimensions other than the human do not matter in landward conflict.[25] But it is unmistakably clear about the primary importance of people.[26] Strategic Landpower is dominated in historical practice today, as it always has been in the past, by the human domain.

Presence and Politics

More often than not in the irregular style of conflict of the 21st century, the strategic value of U.S. Land-power as local presence can be of greater significance than its military worth in the armed struggle. There is a quality of credibility to forward human commitment not reachable with alternative ways and means. This is not to deny that American forward local presence may be akin to a two-edged sword. As a hate object for the focus of hostile attention, the Western soldier on the ground in physically and culturally alien terrain is an adversarial gift as a target to the insurgent. But, if we prove able to raise our game in the field of cultural tolerance—especially given the fact that we will be the foreigners, the Other in local terms to some degree—there is no doubt that the forward deployment of our most highly valued asset, people, carries a message of seriousness of political intent that is universally persuasive.

The point may seem almost too obvious to be worthy of mention, but it is important that we do not forget that our military behavior is always about politics.

In the 2000s, we learned and re-learned a great deal about the domestic politics of Afghan and Iraqi societies, not infrequently as a damaging consequence of our mistakes. This can be perilously easy to overstate, but when we intervene in a hugely foreign country, unless our struggle unavoidably has to be overwhelmingly, not even only primarily, military in nature, we are bound to become intimate, if relatively ignorant, players in local political struggles.[27] Military readers should not be dismissive of the point just registered, because all military endeavor, with its strategic effect, ultimately has to be about political effect. There can be no military or strategic consequences that do not have implications, direct or indirect, for a political narrative. This is not merely an argument, rather is it a definitional truth blessed by an abundance of evidential material, as well as by the philosophical authority of Carl von Clausewitz.[28] If this were not so, then military performance, successful or otherwise in a battlefield sense, would have to be bereft of meaning.

Military deployment and employment is instrumental for political purpose, or even for cultural purpose that will have political meaning. I am suggesting that the forward deployment of strategic Landpower must have unusually intense and probably complicating consequences for the course of local political events, not least because our knowledge and understanding of the informal structures of power in many foreign societies is weak or even near absent altogether. When we join the local fight(s) of others, notwithstanding the seriousness of our own policy purpose, we become active players in violent struggles that have rules and procedures we are unlikely to comprehend adequately for a while. I write this not in order to argue a case against foreign intervention, but rather only to suggest that the very nature of the human domain most characteristic of Landpower all but guarantees that we will need to pay a price in errors committed if we are to be effective in the human domain particular to an alien foreign society. Admittedly, there is much in tactics, and even possibly in operational art, substantially common as sound military practice across frontiers and cultures. But, even the humble corporal, who would be "strategic" in a positive sense, needs to be careful to give the least local offense consistent with reasonable understanding of his duty.

Contrary to appearances, possibly, what I have just written is not intended as a warning against foreign intervention; indeed, if anything, it is an argument generically supportive of the thesis that Landpower is, by its very nature, near certain to have a uniquely strategic effect when forward deployed into an active theater. There is a Janus-like quality unique to Land-power among the whole range of military domains, meaning that this particular, most essentially human kind of military power, has unequalled potential to yield to us either, even both, extraordinary strategic advantage and unusually costly and possibly embarrassingly unsuccessful strategic returns. The deployment of our soldiers into harm's way far abroad should never be treated merely as a routine matter for policy and strategy.

Strategic Landpower and Political Territoriality

Because of the enduring nature of the human domain, every actual, as well as plausibly probable, potential conflict has some territorial definition. Whether particular tracts of land are sought as objects to own legally and politically, or are very desirable for their instrumental value when controlled, there is always a territorial dimension to strategic history.[29] In its very nature, Landpower inherently and necessarily is about land and the resources that exist both in and on it. While seapower, airpower, cyberpower, and nuclear weapons may have deterrent or coercive merit as instruments of strategic influence, Landpower is unique, and indeed essential, as the strategic agent capable of securing and sustaining the political control of territory and its assets.[30] Necessarily as well as obviously, Landpower also is probably uniquely capable of discouraging, defeating, and punishing adversaries on land. This argument does not ignore the strategic utility derivative from joint efforts in support of the narrative on territorial security, but neither is it confused as to who or what must be in the lead for control that lasts on the ground.

It is my contention that, as land animals, humans must and do care most about the land (among all environments). This elementary, indeed simply elemental, truism explains why Landpower has to be regarded as the most vitally strategic of all among the military contenders for highest priority in relative strategic importance. Moreover, it should not escape notice that, even when behavior at sea, in the air, and in cyberspace looms large and perhaps ominously in public consciousness of threat, the anxiety thus produced is translated reflectively into acute concern over landward security. This is unavoidable because all terrestrial concerns need due conversion into analyses and arguments that bear upon our inalienably territorial approach to, and understanding of, national security. Joint military action in and from geographies other than the land occasionally will promote concern or even, in extremis, alarm, but there will always be some territorial reference or implication that cannot plausibly be denied for long.

This monograph now turns to address the joint context within which Landpower must function strategically.

JOINTLY ESSENTIAL, BUT ALSO ESSENTIALLY JOINT

Strategic Landpower is a team accomplishment, with ground forces providing the most defining of characteristic capabilities and behaviors. Specifically, the strategic merit in Landpower derives particularly from the unique ability of ground forces to secure and exploit territorial control of natural and human geography. If the United States needs to send coercive signals, either in warning or in the form of limited but pain-causing actions, then often it will be sufficient to confine our coercive behavior to the sky, the sea, and these days probably also to cyberspace. But, if the putative inimical menace or harmful deeds that are our reason for anxiety or hurt are politically intolerable, then a need may be determined for the effecting of change in the local context.[31] When a situation is perceived as requiring alteration of a nonmarginal kind and is certain to be resisted, with at least some force applied locally, then the political case for the deployment of strategic Landpower will be a strong one. Usually, it will be more than slightly challenging politically for a President to decide to place American boots on foreign ground; this is as it should be because the commitment of Americans to war, or at the least to a warlike prospect, should never be undertaken casually and lightly.

It may be worth emphasizing the fact that the whole context of contemporary warfare is intrinsically and therefore essentially joint in character. Indeed, the character of warfare is now so substantially and necessarily permanently joint that it is appropriate to understand the jointness of the environments for conflict as being so stable as to merit its being understood as an integral feature in the nature of modern conflict. In other words, it is not plausible to anticipate scenarios for future armed conflict wherein American ground forces would not need or want to function in ways enabled by joint effort by a suitable mix of contributions from forces at sea, in the air, in space, and in cyberspace. Even if and when American ground forces are overwhelmingly of particular military and strategic significance, there would be need for support of various kinds provided by military, and also probably some civilian, elements designed to operate in or on geography other than the land.

It is not an important demotion of American Land-power to acknowledge that it is not, and cannot be, synonymous with ground power alone. Co-existing with the world's premier navy and air force may be a budgetary nuisance from time to time, but it is nonetheless a crucially valuable enabler of success for U.S. Landpower. After all, it should not be unduly challenging to the intellect both to grasp the distinction between Landpower and ground forces (or power), and also to recognize the supportive importance of contributions from the extra-territorial geographical environments. Similarly, it ought not to be outstandingly difficult to explain that the most essential mission for American Landpower is the occasional vital need to send American boots to hit foreign ground at times and also in places not always reliably anticipatable long in advance.

Logistics are always of critical importance to national security, and there are excellent reasons why logistical competence long has had to be strongly characteristic of what one might chose controversially to term American ways of war.[32] Bluntly stated, if the American military establishment was not competent in its ability to meet the logistic needs of its forces, the country simply could not fight, at least it could not do so for very long. American geopolitics in several senses quite literally mandated the logistical marvels that have been displayed from the 18th to the 21st centuries. Whatever else may have been less than competitively excellent about American Landpower through more than 2 centuries, challenges to supply and movement almost invariably have been met exceedingly well.[33] An important reason for this generally satisfactory strategic condition simply has been, and remains, American alertness to the implications of raw distance. Not only does the American homeland comprise and consist of territory continental in scale, but global geopolitics located the United States both comfortably and uncomfortably at oceanic distances from the territorial heartland of world politics and strategic history that is and remains Eurasia–Africa.[34]

The joint dependencies that critically help to enable U.S. Landpower to be strategic are not discretionary, rather they are unavoidable reflections of the facts of physical, political, military, and therefore strategic geography. While the dominant ground-force agencies in U.S. Landpower—the Army, Marine Corps, and Special Forces—may own and thereby control with maximum authority and legitimacy, specialized capabilities in fire support, transportation, communications, and intelligence, such particular ancillary aids do not serve significantly to menace the broad meaning or nature of Landpower. Often arguably, it may appear to matter which armed service is primarily responsible for troop conveyance and logistical sustenance of both inter- and intra-theater kinds. But understanding of the nature of strategic Landpower should not be confused by the color of uniform the supportive personnel wear in performing essential joint duty. This is not to attempt to argue foolishly that political ownership of some particular tasking areas does not matter. The military tribes and sub-tribes, despite their essential joint commonality, do each have military cultures that fall short of a perfect match with those most prevalent among "client" Landpower combatants on the ground. Experience of and in distinctive combat roles and duties feeds expectations of support from domains other than the ground that are not surrendered lightly to those whose military culture is likely to be somewhat alien. The most obvious, albeit extreme, example of this phenomenon is the persisting successful determination of the U.S. Marine Corps to own and provide its essential close air support from its own ranks.[35] Marine aircrew are Marines first and aircrew somewhat later. Joint interdependencies endure and are necessary, but they cannot serve entirely to obscure the significance of the facts of geophysics. In other words, each geographical (or at least functional, as with cyber power) domain has to be respected for its unique qualities.

The narrative of strategic Landpower primarily must be one dominated by the course of local events for ground forces. But, notwithstanding military urgency on the ground, provision of joint support from the air requires a permissiveness of weather conditions that will not always be present reliably when and where it is most needed. Even assuming goodwill, honest intention, and strong determination, the facts of diverse geography may reveal rhythms in feasibility that complicate strategic life for the smooth conduct of joint enterprises.

It is well and necessary to remember that a critically important enabling task for joint endeavor is performed by nuclear-armed elements of the forces. These forces, specialized and deployed militarily triadically for potential employment from land, air, and sea (primarily submarines), can play a vital if typically undepreciated role as a deterrent preventive that enables U.S. Landpower to function successfully strategically. Ever since the mid–1950s, American theorists have argued about the extended deterrent worth of nuclear weapons.[36] For our purpose here, suffice it to say that strategic Landpower not infrequently must carry some risk of triggering a great deal more war than the country would like. I must hasten to explain that the nuclear peril may be vitally necessary in order to discourage nuclear escalation on the part of an adversary, while the latent menace in our nuclear posture should help critically to persuade enemies to desist from doing us harm. We can argue about the risks, dangers, and potential benefits of nuclear armament, but there is unlikely to be any clear and definitive strategic conclusion. However, suffice it to say that the U.S. nuclear arsenal serves essentially as a joint enabler for the strategically significant employment of our Landpower. Of course there are risks, "Those that live by the sword . . ." and so forth. Nonetheless, when the American public is invited by rival advocacy groups to endorse and adopt either a version of "minimum deterrence" or the principal alternative—which is close to steady state with our existing nuclear posture—it should be encouraged to recognize that in an increasingly nuclear-armed world, joint performance by Landpower must have nuclear deterrence as a literally vital strategic enabler.[37]

As the concluding issue for this section, it is important to ask whether or not strategic Landpower should be thought of as a category of military power that is approaching its "sell by" date. Not infrequently, the forward deployment of Landpower, if not actually obsolescent as a purposeful strategic act in statecraft, nonetheless has been recognized as so extraordinary a behavior as to merit policy characterization as a "last resort." In his recent book, *Reconsidering the American Way of War*, Echevarria claimed plausibly, that "[a]s the air campaign illustrated [over Kosovo in 1999], the post-Cold War environment did not necessarily suggest that war itself is a last resort for policy, only that the use of land power might be."[38] In the decade of COIN and related behavior, the 2000s, the U.S. Government rediscovered the unique virtues of Land-power as ground power in Afghanistan and then in Iraq, if only in the numerically austere forms deemed appropriate by then Secretary of Defense Donald Rumsfeld.[39]

American Landpower committed geopolitically forward substantially in COIN mode is inherently hazardous; in good part, the peril reposes in the inexorable and potentially strategically weakening effect of the foreign, indeed alien, features of the societies and cultures with which we engage. However, although there are lessons to be learned that should encourage us to be cautious about our ability to help distant friends and allies resist and defeat insurgency, it would be a grave error in policy and strategy were the country to reject any and all missions intended to thwart irregular insurgents. The American body politic should remember clearly enough that COIN was rejected by the armed forces almost mindlessly as a consequence of denial of the Vietnam experience, only to discover that the strategic need for a quality of Landpower able to cope with this kind of conflict, alas, had not disappeared. There was much about the U.S. strategic performance in and over Vietnam that did serve as an invaluable basket of negative lessons, but in vital addition, the country could learn much of positive worth from its protracted adventure there; a like judgment applies quite clearly to our lengthy experience(s) in Afghanistan and Iraq in the 2000s (and a little beyond).

The joint essentiality both of and for Landpower is not in doubt. We know that policy and strategy are driven not only by objective happenings abroad, but also by distinctly subjective political, strategic, and some astrategic sentiments here at home in the United States. Because Landpower is so human in personal, moral, and tangible ways, it is almost uniquely vulnerable to wild swings in what currently is fashionable in "correct" political opinion. When we want American action to be taken, the most seriously committing of possible behaviors is to dispatch some of our human military assets. The fact of "our lives" on the line carries a message of moral as well as political and military seriousness that is unmistakable. All too obviously, of course, the forward commitment of our soldiers unavoidably is also to offer a hostage to strategic fortune. Fashions in political and strategic aspiration and belief come and go, and assuredly will come again. But the future of U.S. politics and policy on security is certain to continue to register as necessary and often dominant role for strategic American Landpower.

CONCLUSION AND RECOMMENDATIONS

This monograph identifies and advances a five-point argument that, in toto, comprises the core of the case for the healthy maintenance of substantial strategic Landpower. This is not, and cannot be, an original thesis, because it reflects appreciation registered by thought and in action over the course of 2 1/2 millennia. That said, it is noticeable how readily people forget, or perhaps just fail fully to recognize the heart of the matter with respect to Landpower. In good part, I suspect rather ironically, a principal reason for some contemporary failure of understanding is only an overfamiliarity with our subject here. Apparently, it is challenging to attempt to have deep and hopefully authoritative thoughts about a concept that in many pragmatic ways is and can be treated all but casually day to day. In this monograph, I have sought to step around both the pressing tactical and technical issues of the day, and also to avoid insofar as I was able the dominant policy-political issues that bear directly upon the Army's future. Instead, I have striven to explore the very nature of strategic Landpower both as it is today and as it should remain tomorrow.

1. **Landpower is unique and irreplaceable**. One of the better terse explanations of the nature of Land-power was provided recently by Brigadier (Ret.) Allan Mallinson of the British Army, when he wrote in *The Times* (London): "Only ground troops can 'smell the battlefield,' discriminate and consolidate."[40] It is important to understand and appreciate the enduring fact that, among all the variety of armed forces, it is only ground troops that systematically make personto-person contact with people—foes, friends, and temporarily bystanding neutrals. Only in land warfare is contact, even personal

contact, made, exploited, and maintained often to the point of a definitive conclusion. Context and narrative may be gained and appreciated from a distance, via photographs, electronic surveillance, or even the old-fashioned printed page, but Mallinson penetrates to the heart of the matter when he cited the opportunity and ability to "smell the battlefield."

There should be no doubt that the danger for a democracy is unique when it decides to deploy its soldiers to foreign lands. However, some of the uniquely politically entangling dangers that can attend foreign deployment may have incomparably high merit also. They provide exactly the personally empirical sources of comprehension that will only be the product of first-hand exposure to foreign cultural patterns and traits. Also, often it is important for the American Soldier not to fade too discreetly into the local natural or man-made landscape. U.S. political commitment of concern for an ally's security typically requires some visible and tangible strengthening evidence by way of the human domain in the form of its soldiers.

Also, of course, it ought never to be forgotten that Landpower by its nature must exert itself upon and within a geography that nearly always includes a foreign population. The vitally important idea of understanding the human domain necessarily pervades all aspects of the mission set for Landpower.

2. **The human domain is an inclusive concept of timeless worth**. Armed conflicts do not appear on our policy and strategy horizons in a standard pattern. That said, as it needs to be, what is standard in and about conflict of all kinds is the dominant importance of the human domain. From the most civilian of domestic politics through to the sharp end of war in its warfare, the human element always is of decisive importance. Even when the possibility of war seems to be related to the balance, or more likely the perceived imbalance, of military strengths between competing arsenals, one finds that human impulse and sentiment tend to dominate cool analytics. The relative significance of the human domain may appear to have diminished with the ever higher levels of technological prowess that characterize international strategic competition, but such a conclusion is inappropriate.

Sometimes we may fool ourselves into believing that we have achieved the ability to peer into the future with reliable understanding. Such belief is as easy to understand as, alas, it is always false.[41] What we do know about the future with complete reliability is that it will be dominated by the free will exercised by often unpredictable individuals. Civilizations, cultures, nations, tribes, and other groups, may well be anticipated to move strategic history along in earnest pursuit of particularly favored narratives, but social science for crowd psychology does not carry high and convincing promise of predictive utility. Athenian historian and (unsuccessful) general Thucydides identified "fear, honor, and interest" as comprising in the barest of inclusive summary form the leading motivations in statecraft. It so happens that what he wrote nearly 2,500 years ago is as true, certainly it is as plausible, today as it was then. Of course, tactical details are nearly always changing, but at the very elevated level of the motives behind and within the politics that produce the policy that needs and sometimes finds expression in strategy, it is not close to self-evident that our human domain today is very different from that of the Ancient Greeks. Similarly, when we consider tactics in the great stream of time we soon discover that revolutions in weaponry have not and probably cannot result in revolution in the personal peril attending, and anxiety concerning, combat.

On the readily accessible historical evidence, the human domain that rules in strategic Landpower in several senses would appear to be all but permanent. Changes in the human military condition have been hugely transformative in appearance, but are far less impressive when we enquire about the nature of conflict through the ages. The particulars of anxiety, fear, ambition, and contingent opportunity vary in rich detail from situation to situation, but as Clausewitz explained in the most summary of forms: "Four elements make up the climate of war: danger, exertion, uncertainty, and chance."[42] He proceeds immediately and deeply into the human domain by arguing that:

> If we consider them [the "four elements" immediately above] together, it becomes evident how much fortitude of mind and character are needed to make progress in these impeding elements with safety and success. According to circumstance, reporters and historians of war use such terms as energy, firmness, staunchness, emotional balance, and strength of character. These products of a heroic nature could almost be treated as one and the same force–strength of will–which adjusts itself to circumstances: but though closely linked, they are not identical.[43]

It seems unmistakable to this author that Thucydides and Clausewitz were writing about a phenomenon of armed conflict common to both of them.

3. **Landpower is always strategic**. The permanent nature of Landpower as a strategic instrument and asset does not mean that always it is so regarded. Military behavior, the activity or passivity of one's Army, cannot help but have strategic meaning. There is no reason in abstract logic or empirical fact why Landpower's strategic quality should be questionable. Given that strategy

is about the consequences of behavior, pre-planned and intended or not, there is nothing extraordinary about the claim that Landpower has to be regarded as a strategic asset. Indeed, this author is somewhat surprised that many people appear to be mentally disturbed in their occasional strategic thinking by the suggestion that Landpower needs to be thought of as an inherently strategic tool of state. However, it is one thing to win a philosophical argument on logical merit, but it is quite another to ensure that that conceptual success influences attitudes and alters relevant behavior.

A significant part of the challenge facing the idea and the practice of strategic Landpower lies in what might be termed the technology overlay that in appearance, at least, seems often to demote the relative importance of "the man on the scene with the gun." It can be difficult to explain to audiences, even to those containing military specialists, that the outcome to armed conflict and its warfare typically is not determined as a consequence of competition in technological sophistication. For a contemporary hypothetical example of argument, we can be sure that there will be no reliable causal connection between a military's sophistication in available computers and its prospects of achieving military and strategic advantage. The reason for this apparently unreasonable argument is because strategic performance and its meaning is influenced by so many variables that even a clear advantage in communication technology is unlikely to be able to compensate for the ill effects of decisions in command and tactical performance that prove to be seriously flawed. In short, technically wonderful computers cannot rescue a strategic adventure that seeks to achieve what is politically, culturally, and possibly even militarily unachievable. This argument is employed here not for the foolish purpose of casting doubt on the military and strategic value of excellence in digital communication, but rather to insist that there is far more to war and warfare than high technology. Regarded prudently as an enabler for strategically and operationally sensible endeavors, there is everything to be said in praise of reliable advanced computers.

Whatever its reactive technical state when competitively regarded, Landpower unavoidably is always a strategic instrument. If this fact is not understood, is disregarded, or is rejected, then the Landpower at issue is likely to be misused as a consequence. The worth of Landpower as a potential strategic asset must vary widely according to the constraints and opportunities allowed by historical circumstance, and somewhat in keeping with the quality in threat and competitively in combat displayed and demonstrated by the soldiers. Due recognition as a strategic asset does not mean automatically and in truth miraculously that our strategic Landpower must be strategically successful in coercive pursuit of policy ends that ought to be politically prudent.

4. **Strategic landpower is always a joint instrument.** Some competition between service organizations and functions is both inevitable and even desirable. It is not unusual for there to be reasonable sounding and looking grounds for approaching a mission in quite radically alternative ways. The tool bag of different military capabilities, human and technical, typically can offer a range of choice. Provided the core human function of Landpower is not sidelined when it really needs to be the central prop for an effort, the feasibility of discretion over ways and means is thoroughly desirable. Certainly, there should be no automaticity of Landpower response to a range of scenario needs that do appear to require local American presence on the ground in question. In point of fact, there are situations when the politics of forward deployment for U.S. ground forces appear to argue in favor of only minimal evidence of presence—in which case, American military assistance from altitude and probably from beyond the horizon at sea is most appropriate.

The central purpose of this monograph is to help ensure that whatever U.S. politics and policy decide is the most suitable strategic response to some local or regional crisis, at least there should be no misunderstanding of the benefits, as well as the probable costs, of Landpower. It is beyond the scope of this monograph to explore and explain the complex connections among politics, policy, and strategy. But, it is important to recognize that Landpower inevitably engages closely either with local politics, or with the consequences of those politics, in ways that are not possible for other instruments of our military power. The strategic function most essentially being about the consequences of military behavior is not itself political in nature, but it cannot help being all about politics nonetheless.

Although the use of Landpower is an exercise in strategy and not in politics, the landward element in our joint ventures ensures that we will engage in contact with local political conditions. Our Sailors and armies in effect can remain convincingly in America in some important senses (e.g., in American "forts" as operating bases), even when their behavior has local effect "in country." The Soldier can be isolated to a degree from local human contact, but we need to remember that personal as well as reputational contact in the human domain of conflict is literally the most distinguishing of the characteristics potentially uniquely valuable about Landpower. American policy does not always desire or require foreign contact and true local engagement in its strategic commitments, but when it does, it is necessary that the merit as well as the possible cost of forward deployable Landpower is well enough understood.

5. **The case for strategic Landpower is as old as strategic history**. Finally, it should be appreciated that the case for strategic Landpower is really as ancient as all of strategic history in the great stream of time. Landpower, one might attempt to argue, is no longer the instrument of final argument of state power, now that nuclear weapons have become permanent elements in some national arsenals.[44] However, the nuclear era was not a decade old before there was quite general recognition that, although the strategic utility of those weapons was high, it was also limited in domain. Indeed, contrary to many expectations fueled by the unsatisfying course and disappointing outcome of the war in Korea from 1950 to 1953, neither conceptual exploration nor subsequent technical innovation served helpfully to render nuclear weapons practicably useful as a strategic instrument.

As a necessary consequence of the practical limitations inhibiting the military and strategic value of nuclear weapons, the United States found itself needing to employ its Landpower as in the days of yore, at least with a pretense of nuclear innocence. In other words, the permanent addition of nuclear weapons to state arsenals, possibly surprisingly, has had only a modest effect upon the strategic utility of Landpower. Of course, Landpower potentially would be sharply disciplined in its use were it to be employed as threat or in battle against another nuclear weapon state.

However, Landpower retains much of its strategic utility, even in a political context influenced by anxieties about nuclear risks and danger. The nuclear dimension to the American joint narrative of military power for strategic effect is real and occasionally, albeit only rarely, immediately important. As a general rule, it is appropriate to consider America's nuclear arsenal being a joint team player whose usual, though essential, duty is to keep the nuclear weapons of other states off the political field of play. With only the blessedly lonely exception of nuclear weaponry, the whole narrative of strategic history is one demonstrating conclusively the essential continuity in the strategic and political meaning and relative value of Landpower.

End Notes

[1] General Raymond T. Odierno, USA, General James F. Amos, USMC, and Admiral William H. McRaven, USN, "Strategic Landpower: Winning the Clash of Wills," *Strategic Landpower White Paper*, no date, p. 7.

[2] *Ibid.*, p. 4.

[3] *Ibid.*, p. 2.

[4] I recognize the fact that the concept of (national) strategic culture is much contested. For good examples of careful challenges to the idea of strategic culture, see Antulio J. Echevarria II, "American Strategic Culture: Problems and Prospects," Hew Strachan and Sibylle Scheipers, eds., *The Changing Character of War*, Oxford, UK: Oxford University Press, 2011, Chap. 23; and Antulio J. Echevarria II, *Reconsidering the American Way of War: US Military Practice from the Revolution to Afghanistan*, Washington, DC: Georgetown University Press, 2014, Chap. 2. Echevarria makes some plausible critical points, but I believe that, on balance, the concept of strategic culture deserves to be saved from comprehensive scholarly slaughter, always provided its perils are recognized, understood, and explained.

[5] Suitably skeptical comment upon the likelihood of there being a continentalist bias in American culture because of the national geography (which changed radically in the 19th century, of course) is offered usefully in Echevarria, *Reconsidering the American Way of War,* p. 39.

[6] I have addressed the much contested subject of strategic orientation in respect of attitudes toward the national geography in my books, *War, Peace and International Relations: An Introduction to Strategic History*, 2nd Ed., Abingdon, UK: Routledge, 2012, Chap. 19; and *Perspectives on Strategy*, Oxford, UK: Oxford University Press, 2013, Chap. 4.

[7] See Holger H. Herwig, *"Luxury Fleet": The Imperial German Navy, 1888–1918*, London, UK: George Allen and Unwin, 1980; and Bryan Ranft and Geoffrey Till, *The Sea in Soviet Strategy*, Annapolis, MD: Naval Institute Press, 1983.

[8] For an outstanding geopolitical and geostrategic analysis that is more than merely an impressive period piece, see Nicholas John Spykman, *America's Strategy in World Politics*, 1942, New Brunswick, NJ: Transaction Publishers, 2007. Spykman is too little read these days, so to help correct this condition, see Colin S. Gray, "Nicholas John Spykman, the Balance of Power, and International Order," *The Journal of Strategic Studies*, forthcoming.

[9] *Army Doctrine Publication (ADP) 3–1, Unified Land Operations*, Washington, DC: Department of the Army, 2012, Glossary-4.

[10] See Colin S. Gray, *Strategy and Defence Planning: Meeting the Challenge of Uncertainty*, Oxford, UK: Oxford University Press, 2014, Chap. 3.

[11] Gray, *Perspectives on Strategy*.

[12] Odierno, Amos, and McRaven.

[13] In his writings critical of America's protracted efforts to achieve counterinsurgent success in Iraq and Afghanistan, former U.S. Army colonel Gian Gentile plausibly expresses doubts about the ability of protracted Western military and other efforts to cope well enough with the pressures, anxieties, and often confusing loyalties encountered in very alien societies. See Gian Gentile, *Wrong Turn: America's Deadly Embrace of Counterinsurgency*, New York: The New Press, 2013. Ironically enough, Stanley McChrystal offers fairly persuasive evidence in support of the thesis that COIN in Iraq and Afghanistan required a level of cultural and political understanding that may be beyond attainment by foreign soldiers in strategically useful numbers. Even in the rare cases of foreigners with adequate cultural comprehension, the practicalities of local deal making and breaking is apt to frustrate attempts to achieve what we consider to be positive strategic effect. See Stanley McChrystal's very detailed memoir, *My Share of the Task*, New York: Penguin, 2013.

[14] J. C. Wylie, *Military Strategy: A General Theory of Power Control*, 1967; Annapolis, MD: Naval Institute Press, 1989, p. 72.

[15] See Richard E. Neustadt and Ernest R. May, *Thinking in Time: The Uses of History for Decision Makers*, New York: Free Press, 1986.

[16] See Harry R. Yarger, *Strategy and the National Security Professional: Strategic Thinking and Strategy Formulation in the 21st Century*, Westport, CT: Praeger Security International, 2008.

[17] Hew Strachan has offered the following cautionary words on the relationship between policy and military action:

Generals who have fought actual wars have found that the presumption that war is a continuation of policy—axiomatic for Huntingdon and reemphasized through a one-sided and selective reading of Clausewitz—has created as many problems as it has solved. Policy, as Clausewitz acknowledged, can be an alien element in war.

"Strategy or Alibi? Obama, McChrystal and the Operational Level of War," *Survival*, Vol. 52, No. 5, October–November 2010, p. 165.

[18] Antulio J. Echevarria II, "Dynamic Inter-Dimensionality: A Revolution in Military Theory," *Joint Force Quarterly*, No. 15, Spring 1997, p. 36.

[19] The importance of control as the object in war is central to Wylie, *Military Strategy*, and is the principal contribution of the book to strategic theory.

[20] The bundle of ideas that emerged in the mid–1950s and matured a decade later on the broad subject area of a desirable flexibility of response in strategy led probably inevitably to the placing of undue faith in the willingness of adversaries to respond, or not, with reliable predictability to American threats and limited military-punitive actions. The whole array of ideas pertaining to limited war in the nuclear age that was triggered initially by reaction to, and reflection on, the war in Korea, fuelled a notably flawed belief that strategic orchestration was possible by clever Americans. The happy, but actually uncomfortably close, outcome to the Cuban missile crisis of October 1962 served to feed the fire of strategic self-confidence imprudently. The allegedly new pseudo-scientific strategy of crisis management was born. This strategic confidence died as a direct result of the Vietnam experience. See Beatrice Heuser, *The Evolution of Strategy: Thinking War from Antiquity to the Present*, Cambridge, UK: Cambridge University Press, 2010, Chap. 17; and Lawrence Freedman, *Strategy: A History*, Oxford, UK: Oxford University Press, 2014, Chap. 13. An exceptionally useful truly contemporary analysis by a leading strategic theorist of the period is Robert E. Osgood, *Limited War: The Challenge to American Strategy*, Chicago, IL: University of Chicago Press, 1957.

[21] In all countries, though particularly in popular democracies, political stability on the home front is an essential requirement that has to underpin, and indeed enable, strategic effectiveness abroad. This point was registered with outstanding clarity in Philip A. Crowl, "The Strategist's Short Catechism: Six Questions Without Answers," Harry R. Borowski, ed., *The Harmon Memorial Lectures in Military History, 1959–1987*, Washington, DC: Office of Air Force History, U.S. Air Force, 1988, pp. 377-388.

[22] Charles Krulak, "The Strategic Corporal: Leadership in the Three-Block War," *Marines Magazine*, Vol. 18, May 1999, pp. 28–34. For an Australian view, not to be outbid by the U.S. Marine Corps, see David Schmidtchen, *The Rise of the Strategic Private: Technology, Control and Change in a Networked-Enabled Military*, Duntroon, Australia: Land Warfare Studies Centre, Australian Defence Force Academy, 2006. Given the widespread popular acknowledgement of the significance of Krulak's argument, it was somewhat ungracious of Smidtchen not to mention his thesis, which had been aired half a decade earlier.

[23] See Colin S. Gray, *The Strategy Bridge: Theory for Practice*, Oxford, UK: Oxford University Press, 2010, Chap. 6.

[24] Echevarria, *Reconsidering the American Way of War*, pp. 41- 42, is plausible in the modesty of his claims concerning the competitive quality of American military equipment, especially for the warfare waged against Germany.

[25] I explore the subject of technological sophistication and combat effectiveness in my *Perspectives on Strategy,* Chap. 5, "Technology: Magic Bullets?"

[26] Carl von Clausewitz, *On War*, Michael Howard and Peter Paret, eds. and trans., Princeton, NJ: Princeton University Press, 1976, pp. 85, 104, 339.

[27] Such unavoidable involvement in foreign domestic politics and their cultural antagonisms are all but thematic in the better of the recent studies of the American and British strategic experiences in Iraq and Afghanistan in the 2000s. See McChrystal, *My Share of the Task*; Jonathon Bailey, Richard Iron, and Hew Strachan, eds., *British Generals in Blair's Wars*, Farnham, UK: Ash-gate Publishing, 2013; and Hew Strachan, *The Direction of War: Contemporary Strategy in Historical Perspective*, Cambridge, UK: Cambridge University Press, 2013.

[28] Clausewitz, *On War*. The pervasive significance of politics is emphasized in Colin S. Gray, *The Future of Strategy*, Cambridge, MA: Polity Press, forthcoming in 2015.

[29] Worded thus, it is easy enough to note the corresponding fit with Thucydides' theory of the three primary motives in statecraft being "fear, honor, and interest." Thucydides, *The Landmark Thucydides: A Comprehensive Guide to the Peloponnesian War*, Robert B. Strassler, ed., New York: Free Press 1996, p. 43. His "fear, honor, and interest" covers more than adequately the reasons behind Vladimir Putin's actively aggressive statecraft and strategy. The Greek general and theorist-historian would have understood Russian policy toward Ukraine with scant need for education in our contemporary detail.

[30] The clearest, indeed almost certainly the definitive, strategic explanation for this is provided with admiral economy in Wylie's *Military Strategy*.

[31] Thomas C. Schelling, *Arms and Influence*, New Haven, CT: Yale University Press, 1966, remains the most impressive theoretical study of coercion in contemporary statecraft. In addition, there is some lasting value in the analyses presented in Lawrence Freedman, ed., *Strategic Coercion: Concepts and Cases*, Oxford, UK: Oxford University Press, 1998. See particularly Freedman's Chap. 1, "Strategic Coercion."

[32] Thomas M. Kane, *Military Logistics and Strategic Performance*, London, UK: Frank Cass, 2001; and Echevarria, *Reconsidering the American Way of War*, are both eloquent on the importance of logistics to strategy. In addition it is well worth noting the judgment of professional military logistician Rear Admiral Henry E. Eccles, USN (Ret.), who wrote explaining that "logistics is the bridge between the national economy and the tactical operation of the combat forces." See Henry Eccles, *Military Concepts and Philosophy*, New Brunswick, NJ: Rutgers University Press, 1965, p. 19.

[33] In his outstanding biography of Dwight Eisenhower, author Jean Edward Smith observes that:

In terms of logistics and supply the maneuvers [U.S. Army in Louisiana, 1941] helped put in place the wartime coordination that distinguished the United States Army in every theater. Lieutenant Colonel LeRoy Lutes, who handled the supply effort of [Patton's] Third Army, became the Army's chief of distribution during World War II and was ultimately promoted to lieutenant general. Lutes ensured that American forces always had more of everything than they might possibly need.

Ironically, perhaps, Eisenhower himself was not known for his logistical skills. See Jean Edward Smith, *Eisenhower in War and Peace*, New York: Random House, 2012, p. 171.

[34] The basic texts are Halford J. Mackinder, *Democratic Ideals and Reality*, 1942, New York: W. W. Norton, 1962; Nicholas John Spykman, *America's Strategy in World Politics: The*

United States and the Balance of World Power, New York: Harcourt, Brace, 1942; and Nicholas John Spykman, *The Geography of the Peace,* 1944, New York: Archon Books, 1969. Notable studies of a more recent vintage include: Ciro E. Zoppo and Charles Zorgbibe, eds., *On Geopolitics: Classical and Nuclear,* Dordrecht, The Netherlands: Martinas Nijhoff, 1985; and Robert D. Kaplan, *The Revenge of Geography: What the Map Tells Us about Coming Conflicts and the Battle Against Fate,* New York: Random House, 2012.

[35] In his fairly frank biography, former Secretary of Defense Robert M. Gates had this to say about the USMC:

But an important reason the Marines deployed to Helmand was that while Marine Commandant Jim Conway was eager to get his Marines off their duffs in western Iraq and into the fight in Afghanistan, he also insisted that all the Marines deployed to a single 'area of responsibility'—one battlespace—with Marine air cover and logistics. Only Helmand fit Conway's conditions. The Marines were determined to keep operational control of their forces away from the senior U.S. commander in Tabul and in the hands of a Marine lieutenant general at Central Command in Tampa. The Marines performed with courage, brilliance, and considerable success on the ground, but their higher leadership put their own parochial service concerns above the requirements of the overall Afghan mission.

Robert Gates, *Duty: Memoirs of a Secretary at War*, New York: Alfred A. Knopf, 2014, p. 340.

[36] See Lawrence Freedman, *Deterrence*, Cambridge, MA: Polity Press, 2004, pp. 34-36; and Patrick M. Morgan, *Deterrence Now*, Cambridge, UK: Cambridge University Press, 2003.

[37] For a sensible contribution to the "minimum deterrence" debate, see Keith B. Payne (Study Director), *Nuclear Force Adaptability for Deterrence and Assurance: A Prudent Alternative to Minimum Deterrence*, Fairfax, VA: National Institute Press, 2014.

[38] Echevarria, *Reconsidering the American Way of War*, p. 149.

[39] See Donald Rumsfeld, *Known and Unknown: A Memoir*, New York: Sentinel, 2011, for the full story from the then- Secretary's perspective.

[40] Allan Mallinson, "The British need to head back east of Suez," *The Times* (London), August 23, 2014, p. 28.

[41] For reasons explained in Gray, *Strategy and Defence Planning*, pp. 17-20.

[42] Clausewitz, *On War*, p. 104.

[43] *Ibid.*

[44] It should not be forgotten that there is often a nuclear context to a local or regional crisis, whether or not nuclear weapon states have sought explicitly to extend nuclear deterrence as cover for the strategic behavior and misbehavior of allies, friends, and perhaps bold neutrals.

INDEX

#

A

B

C

D

E

F

G

H

I

O

P

Q

R

S

T